I first met May some ten years ago through my contacts in the Govan area of Glasgow and was absolutely stricken by her story. It was a period in her life when she was so far down in her esteem that there seemed little hope for her. Drugs and spells in jail were the constant thorns in her existence then from somewhere she found her Saviour in Jesus Christ and her world changed. She decided that the rest of her life would be devoted to saving other unfortunates who were on that same road to self-destruction. She said to me, 'Alex, I'm going to make sure every homeless or anyone destitute will get a free meal every day' and this was the challenge which she has carried out to the letter.

First of all she had the drive and determination to provide a base for her ambitions in Aboukir street just off the Govan road, opposite the Elder park, where many, many lost souls have found their way. And with her charm in raising funds she now has a state-of-the-art building with facilities to execute all her promises.

In all my life I've seldom met a human being with such Christian conviction and caring attitude to her fellow man. Every time I meet her there is this inextinguishable enthusiasm which is so overwhelming that you can only admire and applaud her tenacity to better peoples' lives. May is a star and has a compelling story to tell which will inspire you.

Sir Alex Ferguson, Manager (1986-2013)
Manchester United Football Club

Another page-turner as we are taken into the heart of a world of amazing grace. These are stories which will warm the heart and stimulate tears in equal measure. Truth is so much more gloriously stranger than fiction as we see how God performs miracles in Scotland today. The key is so much more than programmes, May and her friends reveal how the person of Jesus is still as transforming today as he was when he walked this earth. We see that Jesus still walks the streets of the schemes of Scotland through the mouth, hands and feet of his people. You will love the hilarious accounts of the missing chihuahua and the romance which began in the prison cell. You will be drawn into the transformative ministry of Preshal and introduced to a culture where hugs and holiness operate side by side. The depths of sin are reached through the wonderful riches of salvation as you see that there is no such thing as a hopeless case.'

Rev David Meredith
Mission Director
Free Church of Scotland

There is nothing more amazing than to hear true stories of how Jesus saving power can touch and transform people. May has given us another lovely book, filled with personal stories that are not just hers but those who have found love and hope through Jesus at Preshal Trust. What is so powerful are the different ways that God touches people and mends the brokenness within.

There is a verse that comes to mind when I read the books that May has written "Blessed is she who has believed that what the Lord has said to her will be accomplished" (Luke 1:45).

When you spend time at the Preshal Trust Centre you receive the most amazing welcome. The love of God is very present and it's where people can laugh and cry together. This comes through in this book, another treasure that has a story for us all.

Shirley Berry
South West Regional Coordinator
Bethany Christian Trust
Edinburgh

IRENE HOWAT & MAY NICHOLSON

RENEWING
BROKEN
LIVES

**Even More Miracles
from Mayhem**

CHRISTIAN
FOCUS

Copyright © Christian Focus Publications 2015

Paperback ISBN 978-1-78191-685-8
ebook ISBN 978-1-78191-708-4
Mobi ISBN 978-1-78191-709-1

10 9 8 7 6 5 4 3 2 1

Published in 2015
by
Christian Focus Publications,
Geanies House, Fearn,
Ross-shire, IV20 1TW, Scotland, U.K.

www.christianfocus.com

Cover design by Daniel van Straaten

Printed by Nørhaven, Denmark

Contents

Dedicated to the memory of my great friend Cathy, Duchess of Montrose.

Although Cathy was a duchess she was one of Preshal's people and loved us all as much as we loved her.

Foreword

May Nicholson asked me to contribute a foreword to this third book about the Preshal Trust and I count it a privilege to do so. My late wife, Cathy, was involved in Preshal nearly from its beginning in 2002 and the life and work of the Trust went right to her heart. She served as Patron for more than a decade and always claimed to get more from Preshal than she could ever give back to it.

This is the third book to be written about May and the Preshal Trust and that really sums it up. Many charities could have one interesting book written about them. A few might stretch to two, but only a very remarkable work could have a third book written that was just as interesting as the two that went before.

What makes Preshal remarkable? I think that, first and foremost, it is the clarity of its vision. Then it is the love with which the work is carried out and the sheer doggedness of those who serve there and the many others who volunteer. Whatever discouragements they meet, they pick themselves up, dust themselves down, and start all over again.

And why should anyone read a third book about the work of the Preshal Trust? It is as interesting and new as the previous two because it is full of fresh examples of people finding an answer to some of the problems in their lives, and sometimes finding the answer in faith in Jesus.

Cathy and I met through the work of Moral Rearmament. The founder of MRA used to say that he liked to serve 'fresh fish daily', meaning that he liked to have a constant supply of new stories about real people. That's certainly true of Preshal. There is a constant supply of new people coming in the door bringing their stories with them. What does Preshal offer? It offers help that can change tragic stories into hopeful ones, and that is so refreshing.

This book covers the building of Preshal's new home. Cathy and May dreamed about it, talked about it, planned it and had a vision of how it would be used. I am glad that my wife was there to open the new building and to see her vision become a reality.

The word Preshal is Gaelic for 'precious.' And the aim of the Trust is to show everyone who comes in the door that they are precious to God, whether they are someone in search of help, a volunteer passing on a skill or a paid employee of the Trust. It is because all are precious that the place functions as it does. Cathy often talked about 'Preshal's family' and that's exactly what it feels like.

As you read this book you will find things to make you laugh and cry; you may also find some answers to your own questions and a nudge in a new direction. We are all learners and it is as a fellow-learner that I commend this book to you.

Seumas
Duke of Montrose

Introduction

At the end of his letters in the New Testament the apostle Paul sometimes mentions his friends name by name and sends his greetings to them – to Priscilla and Aquila, Epenetus and Mary and so on. In this book you will read about those, name by name, who give their moving testimonies of what the Lord has done for them. You will find here, in the following chapters, May Nicholson's story. More than this, you will find May's story and the story of Preshal interwoven with the stories that men and women tell of their own lives.

Looking back almost thirty years, I remember when May set up the Kairos Group in St Ninian's Church in Ferguslie Park, and the days when the Lord blessed us with a time of revival. Since then I can never read Joel 2:25, where the Lord says, 'I will repay you for the years the locusts have eaten' without thinking of May Nicholson. This was the Lord's promise given to May and fulfilled in her own life. In chapter 1 of this book, May says that her life has been 'a tale of two halves ... the first half was blighted ...' but then she goes on, 'God forgave all that had gone before and made a promise about restoring the years the locusts had eaten. The second half ... has been God keeping His promise.' This is May's personal testimony, but what May says in her own words is there for all to read in Romans 5:10:

> 'For if, when we were God's enemies, we were reconciled to him through the death of his Son, how much more, having been reconciled, shall we be saved through his life!'

At the very heart of the Gospel is the message of sin pardoned and life restored through the Lord Jesus Christ. In Preshal, from day to day, the Lord is at work restoring men and women and building His Church, as Ephesians 4 says:

> 'From him the whole body, joined and held together ... grows and builds itself up in love, as each part does its work.'

For some, as you read this book, there may be moments when you will give thanks to God for His salvation in Jesus Christ seen in lives renewed and restored – the same salvation that you know yourself. For others, as you pick up this book, it may be that through reading it you will find the hope in the Lord Jesus Christ that is often spoken about in its pages, find salvation in Him and hear for yourself too, the promise that the years that the locust has taken away will be restored.

This little book then is, in its own way, a wonderful record of grace – God's grace, for it tells of God's sheer grace shown to us in Jesus Christ, grace unmerited, undeserved, unearned – yet offered to all who will come and receive.

Ian Maxwell
Minister
Uphall South Parish Church
West Lothian

1: Locust Sandwich

My life's like a locust sandwich. It's been a life of two halves with locusts in the middle. Let me tell you how I came to have locusts in the middle of my life.

Half my life ago, in 1981, I was a drunk, a substance abuser and I self-harmed. In a word, I was a mess. I was also the mother of two children. Tracy was twelve and Alan was two. I loved them, I can't tell you how much I loved them, but even when I was sober I knew they didn't deserve to have me as their mum. I used to tell the kids that I loved them so much that I'd give up drink and I meant it every time. But promises are cheap and mine were always broken. My own mum and sister Anne came to their rescue more times than I can tell. And when I was drunk and incapable Tracy and Alan were taken away by them and loved and looked after until I was sober again. It hurts me to say that, but you need to know the truth if you are to understand the story.

When Tracy was eight or nine a crowd of us were gathered together drinking. We had the shakes and sweats and were desperate but we only had two shillings between us. Our eyes lit up when Tracy came in with a miniature bottle of whisky! 'Where did you get that?' I demanded, grabbing it out of her hand. 'I know where there are hundreds of them,' she told us proudly. I was on my feet and scrabbling for two bags. 'Here, Tracy,' I said, 'you go and fill these bags and I'll give you two shillings.' Tracy was up and off. Two shillings was a fortune! When she came back with the bags full of miniatures we fell on them like we'd not had a drop of water for a week and drank ourselves into oblivion. Not long afterwards I met one of my cousins who worked in Grants Whisky near where we lived. He told me that he and his mates regularly stole miniatures and hid them somewhere safe to pick up after work, but that some lucky person (who would not be so lucky if he ever got his hands on him) had found the stash and stolen the lot!

If you've not been addicted, you can't begin to understand the power of addiction. It has you in chains when your mind knows better. Your love for your kids makes you desperate to give it up and, even when you see in front of your eyes the worst that drink and drugs can do, you just can't do it. I remember being with a group of my drinking pals when one of them slit her throat and then fought like a mad thing to stay alive ... until she died, right there in front of us. Addiction is a kind of madness that makes you keep on drinking after you've seen something like that. It blocks out the fact that you could be next.

For years Mum covered up for me. If she hadn't done that, Tracy and Alan might have been taken into care. She did what many mothers of alcoholics and addicts do, Mum made excuses for how I was. I suppose I often went down the line of peace at any price and I was sometimes so out of it that she probably thought I'd kill myself if she took a really tough line. The truth is that the best thing Mum ever did for me was what hurt me most. One day, when she'd reached the end of her tether, Mum slammed the door shut in my face. If I had to give advice to the mother of someone who was like me, I'd tell them to slam the door on their child sooner rather than later.

Tracy and Alan were always well dressed even when I was a mess. Sometimes I was as smart as they were, but that was after a shoplifting spree. I used to shoplift three of whatever I was taking, one to wear and two to sell – to buy more drink, to get more drunk and to make an even bigger mess of my life and theirs. There's a kind of honour even among thieves that stopped me ever shoplifting for clothes for the kids. But I certainly wasn't dressed in the latest outfit on 22nd September, 1981. Tracy was at school when I woke up out of a drunken sleep. Alan was up and toddling around. The poor wee boy was wearing the nappy I'd put on him the previous day.

As I looked at Alan that morning it was as though my eyes focussed, really focussed, on what I was doing to my kids. Don't think I didn't know it before, I did. I knew fine what I was doing, and I'd cried salt tears over them many a time, but somehow that morning was different. I got up, changed and dressed Alan and then wondered what to do and who to go to for help. There was only one person I thought would let me into her house and that's where I went. I wouldn't have let myself in!

As we drank our mugs of tea and Alan toddled around, we talked. 'What are you doing tonight?' I asked her. My friend said she was going to a meeting. 'Can I come with you?' 'No, you can't.' Then she told me some hard truths and didn't stop to spare my feelings. I was a mess. Well, that wasn't news. My clothes were filthy. I didn't need to look at them to know that was true too. They were covered with cigarette burns as well as dirt.

And I smelled. It takes a very good friend or a serious enemy to tell you that you smell. I'd fist-fought with folk for insulting me less than she insulted me that day, but she maybe recognised I was beaten. Either that, or God gave her the insults to punch in my direction because He knew that I needed to hear them.

Now, I was really rebellious from the day I was born. Ask any of my family and they'll tell you that I was the kind of person who couldn't learn from other people's mistakes; I had to make all my own. That day my rebelliousness reared up. If my friend wouldn't take me to her meeting, I'd stand outside her house till she left and then follow her there. Nobody was going to tell me what to do, or what not to do. I followed her from her home in Ferguslie Park in Paisley to the bus stop and then caught the same bus to Glasgow, getting off at the same stop as her. Then I walked behind her along the city streets and into a building. It was a church! Even if I'd realised that before I followed her in, it wouldn't have stopped me. My hackles were up. Because she'd said I couldn't go, I was most certainly going.

I can't tell you how embarrassed I was when I sat down and looked around. I wasn't embarrassed because of the state I was in. For reasons I still can't understand I was embarrassed for all the other folk who were there. Maybe I thought they looked stupid sitting round singing and reading the Bible and praying. Then a man prayed and I remember his prayer all these years later, for it burned into my heart. 'Lord, I pray for that wee woman you've brought here tonight. We can all see that she's filthy by looking at the outside of her, but you know how much more filthy her heart is. Touch her and clean her.' His words could have tipped me into a rage that would have ended in a punch-up, but they didn't. Instead I burst into tears that wouldn't stop. I thought I was so worthless that I wasn't even worth a prayer.

I didn't know till afterwards that it was a Stauros meeting, that nearly everyone there had been an alcoholic and many of them had been just like me. From my point of view we looked as if we'd come from different planets. There was a cup of tea after the meeting and I'd calmed down a bit by then.'Can I have a word with you?' a man asked. 'I'm Charlie Mallone.' We went into a wee room along with another man from the meeting. 'Do you want to be saved?' he asked me. I'd no idea what he was talking about. But I understood when he asked if I believed in God. I certainly did. 'God doesn't want anything to do with the likes of me,' I told him. That's what I believed about God. Charlie was very patient. 'God didn't send His Son Jesus to die for good folk,' he explained. 'He sent Him to die for sinners.'

He was quiet for a minute, and then went on, 'Are you a sinner?' The tears poured down my face and I cried like my heart was broken. 'I'm the worst sinner that ever was.'

I was telling the truth when I said I believed in God even when I was at my worst. Many, many times when I was in prison I prayed and asked God to help me out of the mess. I could have been in for murder for all I knew because I could rarely remember anything about what had happened. And I promised God everything. I'd never drink again. I'd never take drugs again. I'd do anything, if He'd only get me out. When I did get out, my promises were all forgotten with the first drink or fix. I believed God existed, sure I did, but as soon as I sobered up a bit I thought I was too bad for Him to want anything to do with me.

I'd been in psychiatric hospitals from the age of fifteen and even had electric shock treatment when most girls my age were still in short socks. Once I was so high I smashed a prison window, climbed through the broken glass and ran away. When I was caught I was taken right back and put in a straightjacket in a padded cell. If you're wondering what a straightjacket is, it's a jacket with very long sleeves and the sleeves are tied round you so that you can't move your arms at all. Every day Mum walked to the hospital with Tracy to see me. And I remember Dad sitting crying when he visited me there.

Once when Mum was bringing Tracy to see me in hospital my girl went running on ahead. She was as happy as could be and we never knew why until later when Mum discovered that she'd found a wee chihuahua, picked it up, tucked it inside her jacket and taken it home with her! Mum had no idea where it had come from and I don't think Tracy was in the mood for telling her. One of my brothers saw a notice about a missing chihuahua and, guess what, there was a reward for its return. I don't suppose the dog's owner would have paid up so happily if he'd known the whole story!

The men at the Stauros meeting told me about themselves. They'd been alcoholics too, drunks just like me. They said that they were now like blind beggars showing another blind beggar where to get bread. I looked at them and couldn't believe it. They were so respectable! 'I'd love to be like you all,' I said. Charlie explained that God could change me and give me a new heart, if I confessed my sins and asked Him to forgive me. I don't know how long we were in that room together but it was long enough for me to ask Jesus to be my Saviour, to come into my life and turn my whole world upside down – and that's where the locusts come in.

During that night a very peculiar thing happened. A sentence came into my mind, and the words were, 'I will restore to you the years the locusts have eaten.' Now, having been a drunk and a substance abuser my mind was often full of strange thoughts. This was different even though I hadn't a clue what it meant. Locusts could have been a pop band or a football team for all I knew. The next day the words kept rattling round in my head like a tune that won't go away. I spoke to a pastor at Stauros and asked him if he knew what they meant. He smiled and explained that they were words from the Bible. Well, I didn't know anything about the Bible; I didn't even have one. The pastor picked up a Bible, found Joel 2:25 and then showed me the words, 'I will restore to you the years the locust have eaten.' That fairly knocked me sideways! How did I know a verse from the Bible without ever reading it? It could only have come from God. But it wasn't exactly a clear and obvious message!

The pastor patiently talked me though the puzzle. He explained that locusts are insects that, in some parts of the world, fly in huge swarms. When they come to a field with a crop in it they land in their millions and chomp their way through the crop. When they've eaten the lot they rise again in their millions and fly away to search for another crop to devastate.' It's as if the locusts of alcohol, drugs and self-harm have stolen your whole life in the past,' he told me. 'Now God is making a promise that He'll make all that up to you in the future.' What a promise! Before I left the pastor gave me a Bible to take home with me.

Right at the beginning I said that my life was like a locust sandwich, a tale of two halves with locusts in the middle. The first half was blighted by drink, drugs and self-harming and a lot else as well. Then God forgave all that had gone before and made a promise about restoring the years the locusts had eaten. The second half, from 1981 onwards, has been God keeping His promise. The wonderful thing is that this year the two halves are the same length. He has quite literally restored the years, every single one of them, which makes the rest of my life here on earth a bonus!

It was spring-cleaning time, big style, even though it was September. The day after I became I Christian my house was cleaned like it had never been cleaned before. And it needed it! The cheap and rubbishy wine I found in the cupboard was poured down the sink; that was the best place for it. Apart from Communion wine I've never taken alcohol since I became a Christian. I'm grateful to God because He took away my desire for it. Some Christians have a harder time. For reasons we don't understand they have to fight the desire to drink every day for the rest of their lives. We all have different battles to fight.

It's in Tracy and Alan that I see God's promise being kept in the most beautiful way. You see, the locusts didn't just eat away at my life, they ate at their lives too. Tracy remembers what her mum was like until she was twelve years old. I'm grateful that Alan was just two. He knows all about it, but he doesn't remember. If I could wipe Tracy's memories clean, I'd do that. But God has restored my relationship with them wonderfully. Not only that, but I've been blessed with three lovely granddaughters. Leanne is a student and doing really well. Beth and Megan are young teenagers and I love all three of them to bits!

As soon as I was converted I became a missionary. The very next day I went round the doors telling people that they needed Jesus. They must have thought I was on my way home from the pub and out of my mind with drink! One of the first things I did for the Lord was make sandwiches and buy cakes to take to the patients in the psychiatric hospital where I'd been a patient. I had a burning desire to point them to Jesus because I remembered what it felt like to be utterly hopeless. After a while a couple began helping and their ministry grew and grew. They now have a half-way house in Paisley for people coming out of that hospital.

Before long I became an outreach worker with St Ninian's Church in Ferguslie Park, at that time one of the most deprived areas in the whole of Europe. The minister's wife, Ellen, wife of Ian Maxwell, taught me something I needed to learn, and she taught me by example rather than words. She had five children and she always spoke to them softly, and was even quieter if they were doing something wrong. That really made me think. I was a yeller who yelled louder when something annoyed me. Tracy and Alan must have thought I'd tonsillitis when I started to copy Ellen's way of working with her kids. That was probably the first positive lesson I learned by copying someone else.

Months after I became a Christian I met Jessie at the shops. I'd not seen her for a while and she didn't recognise me. When she realised who I was she said that I looked like a different person. That's when I made a theological discovery – impressive! I'd been told that Christians were born again so I believed that I was born again, but couldn't work out what it meant. That day, when I met Jessie, I realised what it meant. I was actually a new person!

The work we did in Ferguslie Park was mostly with people in real need. We made soup and took it to where we knew we'd find folk who were homeless. I welcomed them into my own home too, but I had to be careful about that as my husband wouldn't have been best pleased. He worked shifts, so I told folk when he'd be out and they came for their soup, rolls and tea then. Alan was too young to know what was going on and Tracy was really good about it, though she did ask me not to let them use her cup!

Ellen Maxwell and I ran cash and carry parties. You've probably never been to one! We bought clothes at the cash and carry and then invited people to a social evening where the clothes were for sale at just over cost price and I gave my testimony. This met a number of needs. Women were able to buy clothes they could afford without getting into debt. The money we made mounted up and we used it to support a child in Zambia. And the women who came along heard the Gospel too. In the summer we took them down to places like Largs where we put out tables, set up camping stoves, cooked sausages and burgers and then handed them out as we gossiped the Gospel. You've heard of street pastors? We were early 1980s' beach pastors.

One of my pals in Paisley was called Irene and she had a really effective ministry just where you wouldn't expect it. Her job was to look after the public toilets and she had a wee office there that she kitted out with a kettle, mugs, sandwiches and a Bible. Irene kept her eye on the women coming in and out and, if she noticed anyone was looking upset and tearful, she'd take them into her office and switch on the kettle. Before long her Bible would be open and she'd be telling them about Jesus. I don't know how many women became Christians in Paisley's public toilets, but I know God was working there through His missionary toilet attendant.

Addicts are among the smartest people I know; they have to be to keep ahead of their families. One woman used to let her husband go off to bed and then drink herself stupid on vodka, staggering into the bedroom to join him in the wee hours of the morning. The man told me that he'd searched the house from top to bottom and couldn't find where she kept her drink. One day I asked her where she planked it and said that I wouldn't tell him. She looked at me for a minute and then nodded in the direction of the mantelpiece. 'I fill that up every day,' she said, pointing to a statue of the Virgin Mary. The person who brought it back from Lourdes for her would not have been delighted had she known what it was used for. For all her man would have helped her with her problem, that poor woman didn't manage it and drink destroyed her in the end.

After a while I moved to Dundee to be an outreach worker there. Tracy was engaged to be married and Alan went with me. Boy, was it hard to leave Tracy behind. After three years Alan and I moved back to Paisley and I started work with Glasgow City Mission in Govan. I suppose we were technically homeless as we'd nowhere to go. Even though I knew God would provide, that wasn't a nice feeling. But a friend called Cammie had a wee flat that was going to be left empty when he went to South America for a while and he let us live in it. I believe God allows us to have troubles to turn them into tools to help others. Now when I meet folk who are homeless, especially if they have children, I remember what it felt like to be a number rather than a person with a name. That's how I was treated in the homeless unit and it isn't any better now. Nine years later, in 2002, I left the Mission to establish a Christian outreach called the Preshal Trust in the same desperately needy area of the city.

2: Mum's Purse

Before I became a Christian I wasn't the nicest person to know. Some folk might say that's still true! Certainly not many came to the house door apart from drinking mates and my family checking that Tracy and Alan were alright. But some people didn't have any choice and one of them was my doctor. Drink, drugs and self-harm make for a lethal combination, and nobody knew that better than Dr Jack Clark, who is now in heaven. He wrote a chapter in *Miracles from Mayhem*, which tells my story. I want to quote from what he said there to describe what things were like.

I first met May in my capacity as a local doctor, and calls to her home were not anticipated with any degree of enthusiasm. I recall one late night visit when I arrived to find a real fracas in full swing. May could be quite good at hurtling things around, at doctors too on occasions. When I arrived to make this visit I found the entire tenement brightly lit. The noise was such that nobody around was able to sleep. It was obvious that May had been drinking heavily and she might also have taken tranquillisers. She was bawling and shouting, cursing and swearing. Her house was in utter chaos. It was a very difficult situation altogether, particularly as she had slashed herself, both her wrists and abdomen. As May was pregnant at the time she required immediate hospital admission. Following a time in the acute hospital, she was transferred to the psychiatric hospital, not for the first time. By then she had a long history of alcohol and drug abuse as well as self-harming. May was a woman going nowhere, a poor soul lost in the world.

Years later, much to his surprise, Dr Clark was one of the first to recognise that God was restoring the years the locusts had destroyed.

One night two members of Stauros came to speak at a meeting in my church. … One of the speakers pointed at me and said, "Doctor, you will be able to confirm all that I'm saying." When she saw my incomprehension, she said, "I'm May Nicholson." … I was gobsmacked!

... She was a totally different person. When I knew her previously she was a deeply depressed alcohol addict with no hope and her life was going nowhere. She seemed in utter chaos. ... The transformation in May's life was dramatic ... and God sent her right back to Ferguslie Park to tell the people who knew her as a no-hoper that there was hope in Jesus.

God did send me back to Ferguslie Park and people noticed the change. Even taxi drivers who had often scraped me off the pavement stopped and asked what had happened. And the police noticed too. Before I was converted they used to pick me up blind drunk and then drop me miles out in the country to give me time to sober up on the long walk home. I'd call that compassionate policing; I suppose some people today would call it abuse.

When God took over my life I wasn't the only one that changed. It would break my heart if I spent much time thinking how much suffering I caused my mum over the years. At one point she was so desperate that she and the family decided to get me away from all my drinking pals by sending me to America. I managed to persuade them to make it Jersey instead, for my cousin Tom was there. Because I had a pal in Guernsey I went there first but my 'pal' wouldn't let me in. As I'd no money I went down and sat on the pier to work out what to do next. Two gay guys came along and found me there. They were kindness itself. They took me in, gave me a meal and phoned Mum to tell her I was OK. Then they paid for my flight to Jersey where I met up with Tom.

I was hardly on Jersey when I bumped into some girls from Feegie. They get everywhere! Tom was staying in a men's Model Lodging House and he sneaked us in every night to give us a roof over our heads. Eventually I found a job in a hotel and moved there. I think I must have been searching for something better because I became interested in Mormonism because of a woman in the hotel. For a while I was really into it but the phase passed. One night Tom, one of the Feegies and myself stole a car and headed for Trinity. A police car came up behind us and we thought we'd had it, but the policeman just told us to put our lights on! So we set off again and managed to crash the car through a fence. That was the end of our joyride. Later that night we heard on the television news that the police were looking for two people from Glasgow who had stolen a car and crashed it. Tom and I were off the island before they had a chance to put a check on the port. Years later Tom became a Christian too.

From Jersey I went to Blackpool, arriving there broke and with nowhere to sleep but the streets. I was at rock bottom, the lowest I ever was. Penniless, I ate what I could find in bins and slept on the streets. I was so out of it that I don't know how long I was there. But eventually I phoned Mum's neighbour, reversing the charges, and told Mum where I was and that I wanted to come home. Did she say, 'Away you go! You've broken my heart once too often'? No, she did not. She said I'd to go to the GPO and she'd transfer the bus fare home. My wee mum hated the sin but she loved the sinner. And when I reached home she had the water heated for a bath and a meal ready for her prodigal.

In the story of the Prodigal Son, Jesus tells us that no matter where we go, no matter what we do, no matter how deep and dirty the hole we dig ourselves into, the heavenly Father is always waiting with His arms wide open to welcome us home. And we're welcome home because He sent His only Son, Jesus, to take all our punishment, to wash the dirt of all our sins away and make us clean enough for heaven. There's not a person in the whole wide world that I would give my daughter or my son for, but God gave His Son to die on the cross for you and for me.

I'm so glad Mum lived to see the change God made in me. After I'd been a Christian for a while she even gave me a key to the house. Unless you've been in a situation like that, you'll never know what that meant to me. Preshal exists for people like me, people who have never been trusted even by their closest family. One of them is Martin and he'll tell his own story.

MARTIN'S STORY

I was the youngest of a family of four boys and we had a happy home. Dad and Mum worked hard. Mum was a cleaner in the police station. The first time I tried drugs was when I was nine and it was magic mushrooms. My brothers gave me them and thought it was funny. I left school with no qualifications. When the others were choosing their subjects in second year, the teacher said I'd not been there often enough to choose, so he gave me a football and told me to go outside and have a kick-about. We all sniffed glue but I knew my brothers were into Heroin and before long I was too. Heroin was all over the place.

I remember coming home from school one day to a bit of an upheaval. It turned out that one of my brothers had been sent to prison. From then on the police seemed to come to the house often. That must have been awful for Mum because she knew the police. I started selling drugs when I was about nineteen to feed my own habit. A boy in the housing scheme asked me if I wanted to sell for him. And it wasn't always money in exchange for drugs, sometimes it was sex. Looking back I'm ashamed of what I did and having three brothers doing it before me is no excuse. I knew what I was doing. At my 21st birthday party, one of my brothers told me he was going to London the next day. Shortly afterwards, two policemen arrived at the door to tell Mum that he was dead. He'd broken into a chemist and then fallen down a stair when he was high on stolen drugs. He was found by a man out walking his dog.

One day Dad checked my jacket and found some Heroin in my pocket. When I discovered what he'd done I went round and punched him in the face. Dad went missing one day. He had been knocked down when he was walking through the Clyde Tunnel; he was drunk at the time. Dad was in hospital for ages and was never the same man again. It was really sad. He's dead now.

Over the years I just got deeper and deeper into the drug scene and eventually had a nervous breakdown. That was when another of my brothers was found dead in a close in Govan. He'd been clean of drugs for ten years when he met some friends, took something and died. And do you know what his 'friends' did? Instead of dialling 999 and getting help, they phoned for a Chinese carry-

out so that the delivery man would find him. Time went on and things only got worse. In 2013 Mum came to where I was living to tell me that my last brother didn't look well. I went round to his house and found him there, dead. I started off the youngest of four brothers and now I'm the only one left. I have a wee boy and I have custody of him because his mum is on drugs. So was I when he was born. In fact, while his mum was in labour I was full of ecstasy. He was born on Christmas Day and somebody gave me a present of a bottle of whisky. Not a great idea.

I was still doing drugs when I first came to Preshal. I could see that the people here were different. After a while I began going to the Bible study that takes place every week and I gave my life to Jesus. Before that I always walked looking down at the ground and being a Christian made me look up. I go to the Fellowship Meeting on a Sunday night too and learn a lot there. I've taken friends to that and one of them has become a Christian.

Over the years I must have stolen thousands of pounds from my mum, and she's never had money to spare. I used to rake around the house – hunting for any tablets that the doctor had prescribed for her to see if they would give me a high. Not long ago I asked Mum for a loan of some money and she told me to give her over her handbag. You've no idea what it felt like to be trusted. Till then she had always hidden it away. Now if I need a pound or two she hands me her purse and lets me take it out. I'm still not used to being trusted. I've been invited to a wedding this year. I've never been invited to one before because everyone knew I would drink too much and probably end up fighting. It feels strange now being invited to places with Mum.

I go to the Church of the Nazarene and for a while I helped with the youth work there. I couldn't believe it when the pastor gave me a key. I suppose I'll get used to feeling trusted one day, but it will take a while. My son and I live round the corner from Mum and we go there for our dinner every day. I don't really have many friends because most of them have passed away. I've lost count of the number I've lost to drugs and drink, and that's as well as all my brothers.

Coming to Preshal is one of the best things I've ever done and I'm going to keep coming. I found it really hard to come in the door the first time but you get to know people really quickly and the members of staff are great. There's always somebody to talk to. Until I came here I didn't think I was worth anything. I'd never seen a Bible until I saw one at Preshal; now it's my favourite book. Mum comes too. She has stuck by me all the time. Mum's been a rock, always there. I hope I'll always be *there for her especially because she's not got anyone else now since all my brothers have died. She's had a really hard life.*

MARTIN'S MUM'S STORY

My husband and I brought up our four boys in Drumoyne in Glasgow. We had a nice home and were there for 21 years. My man was a good father and strict with the boys. But all four of them got hooked on drugs when they were young. That was what happened to nearly all the boys round about us. The eldest, Robert, went to London and told us not to worry and he'd be alright. He was only down there for a week when he died. He'd taken Heroin and his so-called friends put him out the flat. But he fell down all the stairs and was so badly injured that he died.

Andy, he was the next one down, died five or six years later. I'd gone to Canada on holiday and was away when he died. He'd been off drugs for years. Sadly he went out drinking for a week and maybe someone injected him. I don't know what happened but he died anyway. Then there was Stephen who was a lovely boy. He came off Methadone and was doing well. He stayed round the corner from me and I used to give him his dinner every night. One Saturday he went out for a wee drink. I went up on the Sunday when he didn't come round and found him in the hall. Martin discovered that Stephen was dead.

Martin's the only one left now. When he was on drugs all I did was worry about him. We heard of Preshal a while ago and we've been coming for four or five years. It's a great place and they help a lot of people. They've certainly helped Martin and they've helped me too. When I think about my boys that have died I just wish they had come here too. Things might have been different then.

When some people become Christians they are delivered from their addictions right away. Drink doesn't trouble converted alcoholics and drugs or gambling doesn't tempt former addicts. They are very fortunate. There are many true Christians who are tempted by their addictions for the rest of their lives and that makes it very hard for them. God must have His reasons and maybe it helps them to understand others. But in between the two extremes Christians who have been addicted sometimes go forward five steps and back two, or maybe six. Or they get on really well for a while and then are suddenly taken by surprise by temptation and give into it before they realise what's happening. That's the devil trying to make a mockery of their testimony. The temptation is to cover up but that never works. It just adds sin to sin and digs a deeper hole for them to fall into. God's waiting to forgive.

If I'd not become a Christian, I'd have gone the way of Martin's brothers and my mum would have mourned for me like Martin's mum mourns her three boys. The first half of my life was just like theirs. I had a good home and strict parents. Dad and Mum were grafters; they needed to be to keep us all, for we were a big family. Although we were poor we didn't know it because everyone around us was just the same. It's different today. Poor children now know what they don't have because they see it on television.

Preshal is the Gaelic word for 'precious' and we hope that everyone who comes in the door feels accepted and precious. Our greatest hope of all is that those who come in will discover that they are precious to God, so precious that He sent His Son Jesus to die on the cross to save them from their sins. It was the locusts of my sins that destroyed the first half of my life. It wasn't my upbringing, it wasn't my dad and mum's fault, it wasn't poverty, it was all my bad choices put together.

We don't preach to the people who come to Preshal but we don't make any secret that we're Christians. When friends do become Christians we encourage them to talk about Jesus and to tell others about Him. So it's not unusual to hear people sitting round a table talking about the Lord while they drink their coffee and eat their morning toast and butter. Yes, butter. Preshal's people are precious and they deserve butter rather than margarine!

Since Preshal began, in 2002, hundreds of people have come through the door of the different buildings we've been in. Now we have our own purpose-built centre and over 450 people make use of it. There was a time in my locust years when I was sleeping rough on the streets of Blackpool. Today I come to Preshal's beautiful new building and welcome others that I know have slept on the streets just like me. God has certainly restored the years the locusts ate in a very wonderful way.

'The truth is that May would not be able to do the work she is doing now if she had not been through the things she went through. ... When we began our relationship I was a doctor who dreaded a call-out to May's address, and she was a patient in dire straits and not always welcoming. Now we are brother and sister in Christ ....' (the late Dr Jack Clark)

3: Leaving the Past in the Past

When I was young the only friends I had were drinkers and drug addicts. Nobody else was interested in us and we weren't interested in them either. Sadly drinking friends are only ever best friends with those who have money in their pockets. True friendships were among the things that the locusts of drink, drugs and self-harm stole from me and over the years since I've became a Christian God has just showered me with really good friends. Libby, who has been a friend since Preshal was just a baby, shares her story.

LIBBY'S STORY
May's right saying that I've known her since Preshal was a baby because a friend and I went in the door of St Kenneth's Church hall very soon after May opened it. But my story

begins a long time before that and what
Preshal means to me will only make sense if I
start right at the beginning.

When I was six years old my young brother
was murdered. That was a day I will never
forget. We were getting ready in the morning
when my wee brother went out. He was nearly
two years younger than me. Mum went to find
him and took me with her. Not far from home
we found him lying with a hatchet embedded
in his head. He was dead though we didn't
know that. He'd been killed outright. I don't
think I have ever been truly happy again since
that day.

People cope with tragedies like that in
different ways, or don't cope. And it's a
fact that after a child's death couples often
part company. I suppose it's because they
deal with it in different ways and just grow
apart. Whatever the reason, Dad and Mum's
marriage broke up and he went away. Before
very long Mum married again. If I was a sad
little girl before my stepfather arrived on the
scene, I was a miserable and scared one after
he came. I disliked him as soon as I met him,
which couldn't have been easy for Mum. I had
good reason to dislike him.

Sexual abuse of children is reported in the
papers these days but I can vouch for the fact
that it's nothing new. My stepfather's abuse
was total: physical, emotional and sexual. He

was an evil and a powerful man and I was a child. Put like that it's obvious that I wasn't responsible for it but I was the one who felt dirty and guilty ... and terrified. People like him are very clever and he managed to do what he did to me without Mum knowing. You wouldn't think that was possible but, if someone is determined to do evil things, he'll find ways of doing them.

Mum had her own troubles because my stepfather was guilty of what today would be called domestic violence. That's all over the papers nowadays too, but it's not new either. It was the big thing that people didn't talk about when I was a girl. I remember many a time when he picked a fight with Mum and then started to lash out at her. My sister and I would stand in front of her in the vain hope that would stop his punches. It didn't, but at least he hit us rather than her. You can't begin to imagine the excuses people made for cuts and bruises. Women would say that they'd tripped and fallen against the dresser or slipped and clattered down the stairs. But everyone knew the signs. It was the great unmentionable.

I managed to get away from home by the quickest means possible. I went to train to be a nurse which, in those days, meant staying in a nurses' home. Some of the trainee nurses fought against the rules and regulations; I loved them. I was free of that evil man and I was safe. Then I met Andrew and we married young. Strangely a lot of abused children go on to marry men who abuse them. Andrew wasn't like that at all. Our romance was like a Mills & Boon novel. We met in hospital where he was a male nurse and at last I felt safe and loved. Andrew didn't come between me and my mum. She and I were always very close. Very soon we were blessed with a lovely daughter called Jackie. She was, and still is, the love of my life.

I remember the day Jackie was born. Mum came up to see me in the hospital. 'Are you sure this is your daughter?' she asked, because our family are all dark-haired and Jackie was fair like Andrew. It was a strange thing, but although Mum knew I was happily married she never once called Andrew by name. He was always 'him'. I think her experience of my stepfather had soured the way she thought about men. Who could blame her?

My poor mum died of cancer; she died in my arms on a Monday. That Saturday my step-father died and seeing Mum's grave reopened so soon and his coffin laid on top of hers was just too much for me to bear. Very soon afterwards I suffered a nervous breakdown and was off work for about a year. When I did eventually go back to work it was just part-time and I still suffered from depression. I felt down all the time and so lonely. Even though

I had Jackie I still felt completely alone in my sad little world. My depression wasn't helped when my marriage broke up and Andrew left.

I was always looking for things to comfort me and once I went into a Bible shop to see if there was anything there. That day I found a copy of Footprints and it gave me such a feeling of happiness that God was actually with me, even in the bad times.

'One night a man had a dream. He dreamed he was walking along the beach with the Lord. Across the sky flashed scenes from his life. For each scene he noticed two sets of footprints in the sand. One belonging to him and the other to the Lord.

When the last scene of his life flashed before him, he looked back at the footprints in the sand. He noticed that many times along the path of his life there was only one set of footprints. He also noticed that it happened at the very lowest and saddest times of his life.

This really bothered him and he questioned the Lord about it.

"Lord, you said that once I decided to follow you, you'd walk with me all the way. But I have noticed that during the most troublesome times in my life there is only one set of footprints. I don't understand why, when I needed you most, you would leave me."

The Lord replied, "My precious, precious child, I love you and I would never leave you!

During your times of trial and suffering, when you see only one set of footprints, it was then that I carried you."'

I was brought up a Catholic and had always gone to church. That side of my life was important to me. In fact, I couldn't have got through what was thrown at me without the support of my church. One day I started a new spiritual journey without even realising it. I was out with a friend and we were looking for somewhere to go, preferably to do with art. I like arty and crafty things. We were walking past Preshal and decided to go in there. It was in the very early days. The new Preshal has very comfortable premises with a beautiful kitchen. Then Preshal met in a church hall and the catering facilities equalled one kettle and one toaster. The menu was simple. There was tea and coffee, toast and butter. And nothing ever tasted quite so good!

It was through Preshal that I became a Christian and my life changed completely, especially with the help of the weekly Bible studies. Jesus is my closest friend and May is my best friend on earth. I thank God for her. She has a soft heart but she's not scared to be hard if that's what's going to help you. And she's not frightened to tackle hard subjects that other people might steer clear of. I can't tell you how much I appreciate that.

May goes out speaking at meetings a lot and she usually takes some Preshal people with her. One night I went along and heard her speaking about forgiveness. She was talking about the years the locusts had eaten and about God giving her those years back. I suddenly realised that I was still letting the locusts eat away at my life by still bearing the pain of my abusive stepfather. Right there and then I decided to forgive him, to let the past be past, and not to let it spoil whatever future is left to me. I'm not the Libby I was before that night. God has opened my eyes to deeper and deeper things and I've discovered, and keep discovering, the joy of being forgiven and of forgiving.

When my stepfather died I fell out with my sisters because I didn't want his remains to be buried in the same grave as my mum. For many years there was no contact between us and no friendship. But Preshal has helped to bring us together again and I'm really grateful for that. Now we meet up here and see each other most weeks. And I'm ending my story with a smile. Preshal has a caravan down on the coast at Saltcoats and I love going there. That's my time-out place. And when I'm sitting outside the caravan just yards from the beach, I sit there and think to myself, 'This is what I was born for.' Just imagine what it will be like in heaven!

May

Preshal's people, folk like Libby, are friends
with each other and they're also my friends.
Even outside of Preshal they are still my friends;
I don't go home and forget them. True friends
are genuinely interested and listen when each
other speaks. My friends in Preshal are as
interested in me as I am in them. And never
was that more true than when I had cancer
some years ago. You find out who your real
friends are when something like that happens.
We're beholden to each other and that's what
makes healthy relationships.

4: Lonely in a Crowd

On the morning of the day I became a Christian the only friend I could think to go to was so ashamed of me that she wouldn't even take me with her to a meeting of former alcoholics. Now, you don't get much lower than that. It wasn't that Ferguslie Park was an unfriendly place. That was absolutely not true. It was just that I'd worn out any friendships I had by my drinking, drug-taking lifestyle.

Let me tell you what Ferguslie Park was really like. The flat I was born in was like thousands of others in Scotland at the time. It was a 'room and kitchen'. In the room there was a curtained-off recess and behind that there was a built-in bed. I was born in that bed and all my brothers and sisters were too. I was three or four when we moved into a brand new house in a newly developed part of Ferguslie Park. It was the biggest housing scheme in Europe at that time. Nowadays children brought up in social housing schemes are nicknamed 'sceemies', and it's often used as an insult. In my day we were 'Feegies' – and proud of it! In our posh new house we had two bedrooms, a kitchen and a bathroom and we thought we'd joined the gentry! We were a bit overcrowded but my Aunt Lizzie, who lived next door, was even more so. My aunt and uncle had seventeen children!

We lived a kind of communal life with our cousins and we didn't even go outside to meet up with them. There was a hatch in the hall floor and, if we hopped down there, we just needed to grope our way through the darkness under the house until we came to the hatch in their hall. A quick thump on the bottom of it soon brought one of our cousins to open it up and let us in. Sometimes we went further along and banged on other folks' hatches. Until they got to know us they probably thought their houses were haunted!

The late Dr Jack Clark described the area where I grew up:-

The Ferguslie Park area of Paisley was developed in the late 1920s and early 1930s to give people good housing that was to greatly enhance the quality of their lives. The streets were well laid out and the buildings good quality. Most were tenements and were two or three storeys high, though there were a few with four storeys. The first tenants came from the old central tenemented area of the town, from housing built round the mills to house the workers. The mills then employed about 13,000 people. It was like the end of a football match when the mill horns sounded and the shifts changed.

This housing development should have been a success but it failed to reach its potential and ambitions. Folklore had it that some people kept coal in their baths, and doors could on occasion provide emergency firewood. Alcohol became a problem, and poverty was real. But in the midst of it all there were some fantastic people, families with real ambition to better themselves. Although there was a problem with violence when I was a young doctor I never felt threatened.

Some years after the Second World War considerable unemployment became an increasing reality. Drink was a persistent problem. Within a few decades Ferguslie Park changed from a hopeful new housing scheme to an area marked by despair. In the 1950s, when May was a child, more housing was built and she moved from one of the older houses to a new block.

May's generation of children in Ferguslie Park was often poorly nourished, and not through maternal neglect. A high proportion of income was spent by men in the public house before going home on a Friday night, if they were in work and, if they were not, their wives were fighting a losing battle to keep their children well fed and decently clothed. At that time to be poor meant to be really poor. Having said all that, many of those who did live there were survivors. The area produced winners and losers, and the winners were strong, strong people. They had to be.

MAY

That was how our doctor saw Ferguslie Park. How we saw it was different. He knew we were poor; we didn't because nobody told us and everyone was the same, and we didn't have televisions to see how the other half lived. Dr Clark knew we were overcrowded; we didn't because we had a lot more space than we'd had in the room and kitchen where I was born. The doctor recognised we were undernourished; we didn't because we had nothing to compare ourselves with. Nowadays I eat my meals because it's meal time. When I was a girl I ate meals because I was hungry, and sometimes I was hungry for a good while before it was time to eat.

There's one part of Ferguslie Park that Dr Clark didn't mention and I think it was there that the rot set in that eventually gave the place the bad reputation it came to deserve. The council chose a cul-de-sac in the scheme and allocated the flats there to people who didn't look after their homes. It's almost unbelievable in our politically correct day and age, but these people were called 'the undesirables'. I think it was a case of 'if you give a dog a bad name ...'

You might have noticed that Dr Clark didn't mention Ferguslie Park being a lonely place. It wasn't. There were always dozens of kids out in the street playing. Now children sit alone in their bedrooms with their PlayStations. Not every family lived in the kind of community we did with our underfloor tunnel system to our cousins! But everyone lived in community. When our hair needed cutting one of the local women came with her scissors. Our week-to-week 'hairdressing' involved us sitting on a chair that had a sheet of newspaper underneath it in order to have our hair tugged through a steel comb to dislodge any resident nits. These fell on to the newspaper which was screwed up and thrown in the fire. If we wouldn't take our medicine, there was a woman who knew the 'hold the nose, force the mouth open and pour it down the throat' method of administration. If Wee Johnnie (or, more likely, Wee May) had been up to mischief, news travelled through the bush telegraph more quickly than Wee Johnnie could run home.

When someone died the people round about arrived to do the necessary: one to take the children away, another to help lay out the remains, someone with a pot of soup, others with the promise of sandwiches for the funeral and one or two to help clean out the house before the formalities began. And there would always be enough offers of the loan of black clothes for everyone in the bereaved family to be suitably dressed for the funeral. We were deprived of a lot of things, but we were never lonely. We were hardly ever alone and that suited us fine.

Today people can be living in the same close and pass each other on the stair without even saying hello. Children don't run about with other children. In the area around Preshal you hardly ever see kids out playing in the street or in the park. Parents are frightened to let them out of their sight. Even if they're not scared of people hurting their kids, they'd certainly be worried about them picking up a syringe and jagging themselves with it. And older people can be really lonely, especially if they are living on their own. My mum had loads of problems to cope with in her life, but I don't think she could have told you the meaning of loneliness.

Jimmy's story

I'm a Govanite but I moved to Pollock when Cathy and I were married, and then to Pennilee. But if you're born in Govan, you're always a Govanite. I married a good wife and we had two sons. She died in 2007 and I still miss her. I was seventy-two when Cathy passed away and I just went into my shell, sitting in the house watching television all day, every day. I felt that I'd nothing to live for. I'd had a border collie for sixteen years but, because he died the year before Cathy, I didn't have any need to go out the door.

One day my older son came in and said that I had to make the effort to get out and see people. I told him I'd no notion of that. But he said he was going to get me another dog and then I'd need to go out to walk him. We got a dog from the dog and cat home and he was a winner. I have problems walking and he seemed to know that. If I walked, he walked, and if I stopped, he stopped. He wasn't very intelligent but he was very obedient and that's what matters in a dog.

After six years that dog died and I went right down into depression. My sons were worried about me because I stopped going out and didn't want to see people. One Saturday

I had to go to Govan and I saw a notice that said, 'Do you want to learn new skills?'

I went in and discovered that it was a welfare shop and I knew the woman who ran it. She told me about Preshal and said it was just the business for me. It took a real effort to go the first time but that was a year ago and I look forward to coming now. My sons say that it's the best thing I've ever done.

I love Preshal and everyone in it. A stranger coming in here feels like they've been before. I used to come on Mondays, Tuesdays and Thursdays. But I've changed my routine now. Wednesdays used to be my housework day but now I come here then too. I would really recommend Preshal to anyone who is lonely and needs companionship. And it's for everybody. Disabled people fit in and so do those with learning difficulties. There are people of different religions and different colours. Everybody's here. Two days a week there's a lunch club. We get a lovely meal. I'm never ready for my tea when I go home these days!

I've been in Preshal for a year now and I hope I'm fit to come till the day I die. I believe in Jesus although I don't go to church. This is a Christian club and I like that side of it. It's made me think about what I believe even though nobody pushes the Bible down your throat. It's just that people talk about what they believe. I've never been in a place where that happened before. You're not forced to go to religious lessons or anything like that. Everything's optional here; nobody is forced to do anything. I go along to the sewing group and I love it!

May's a wonderful person and I think she does a great job. What I notice is that Preshal is very well run but it doesn't look as if anyone is running it. That's because the team works together and they can't do enough for you. My sons are happy for me to come to Preshal. They say it's a pity I didn't go before. One of them told me that they used to never be able to get me out the house and now they can never get me in! My one regret is that I didn't come here years ago and that my wife was never here to enjoy it. She would have loved it too.

BARBARA'S STORY

When I was working I enjoyed being with older folk and now I'm one of them myself. I was brought up in Govan and am back here again now. By nature I was a hard grafter and was eleven years cleaning in a nursing home. I think they liked me there because I did a good job and could blether to anybody. We all had our own bit of the building to clean but I used to do the communal areas too. If they couldn't find me, they just looked in odd corners for my cleaning trolley and I'd be there scrubbing or polishing.

When I was seventy-five I had a stroke; that was a couple of years ago, and now I can't do the things I used to do. I'm not able to do the likes of putting up curtains, so I just wait and ask my son (I have two sons) and he doesn't even need a ladder to do it! But I don't get down about things; there's no point in sitting around moaning. After I had my stroke I was to get a carer to take me out. After two days, when nobody had come, I went out for a wee walk myself and managed to get from my street to the subway and back. When I reached home I was so tired I just went to my bed. Next day the woman came and said that she was sorry she couldn't get someone to take me out. I told her what I'd done. She was amazed and said she thought I'd only manage round the building. I was fair pleased with myself!

I tried to have a bath and that nearly ended in disaster. First of all I tried getting in and out the bath with no water in it and managed to do that. So I ran the bath, got in … but couldn't get out again. I have an emergency cord in the bathroom and thought I might have to pull it. But I knew what would happen if I did; they would send for the fire brigade and firemen would come and lift me out. I wasn't having that if I could possibly help it! I sat in the bath and tried to puzzle it out. Then I remembered that I'd managed in and out when the bath was empty. So I pulled out the plug and let the water drain away and then struggled out. I didn't want to be rescued by firemen!

Someone asked me if I'd like to join a wee club and that's when I came to Preshal. The first day I sat beside a nice woman who called me Granny Barbara because I reminded her of her granny. That was nice. We got on well but she died not long ago. I come Monday to Friday each week. It's like a full-time job! It's made such a difference to me that my sister says she can tell the difference even over the phone. I get up every morning and look forward to what's happening that day. I've done all sorts of things at Preshal that I've never done before, even though my fingers are not so good these days. When I get home about 4.30 pm I just have a cup of tea and a sandwich and settle down for the evening.

On Thursdays I go to the Bible study that Sheila takes. Even if I forget my glasses, I can still listen to what's being said and I've learned such a lot about Jesus. Sometimes what Sheila says goes out my mind but I think it stays in my heart. We take our tea in with us to the Bible study and drink it while we listen. Some people talk but I'm a listener. I've really liked learning about Jesus. So that's the story about how I came to Preshal at first and why

I'm happy every morning to go out and catch a bus to come here again and again.

MAY

The friends that the locusts of sin stole from me have not only been restored in my life but through Preshal many, many people like Barbara and Jimmy have found friendships that are precious to them and that brighten their days. My prayer is that Preshal's friends will come to know the best of all friends, the Lord Jesus Christ.

5: Tough love –Times Two

I always felt like the odd one out in the family when I was a girl. In fact, I sometimes wondered if Dad and Mum were my real parents because I was so different from my brothers and sisters. As my life went from bad to worse I think they too wondered how they could be related to me. I didn't fit in at school either. The first time I felt at home in the world was when I was fifteen and working in a café in Paisley. One day another girl who worked there asked if I'd like to share a half bottle of wine with her. I said I would though I'd no idea what wine tasted like. We went up an alley and she took the first drink and then handed the bottle to me. I took two mouthfuls and stood there – amazed. The warmth that ran down my throat seemed to go straight to my mind and heart, melting everything inside me and making me glow.

All my insecurities melted as well and I stood there at peace with the world for what felt like the very first time in my life. Before we finished that half bottle of wine between us I was an alcoholic. I was a different person and I was hooked. Not long afterwards I discovered that drugs could give me the same warm glow, the same peace, the same relaxation and the same great feeling of fitting into the world. Even if I'd known the damage I was going to do to myself, I don't think I could have stopped. I liked the new person that drink and drugs made me and I had never liked the old me without them.

Until 1981 I went further and further along that road until the day I met Jesus, the day He promised to restore to me the years the locusts had eaten. One of the ways in which He has done that is by bringing young folk to me who need the kind of help I needed and didn't get for many years. One of them was Shona. She arrived on the scene just about the time Alan left home. I've heard of empty-nest syndrome, but I didn't have time to find out what it meant. In fact, I barely had time to change the sheets!

SHONA'S STORY
I was brought up in a happy Christian home and knew right and wrong from when I was a

wee girl. Going to church was part of family life and I kept going as a teenager just to keep Dad and Mum off my back. Unfortunately the life I led during the week wouldn't have pleased them if they'd known about it, and maybe they did. I started drinking and smoking and became a single mum when I was sixteen years old. I didn't realise it but I was just a kid myself. There was never any question of giving up my son. I loved him!

My boyfriend and I tried to make a go of our relationship and we had another baby boy about eighteen months later. But it didn't work out for us and we split up. Somehow I got by with the help of my family but inside my head things weren't good. My self-esteem was at rock bottom and it was as though the devil played a tape in my head that told me over and over again that nobody would want me, a single teenaged mum with two wee children. Everything about me said that I was in the depths. I even walked with my head held down rather than looking up and out at the world.

Some time later, I got into another relationship which seemed good at first. My boyfriend had plenty of money and the boys didn't want for anything. We had a comfortable home, fancy clothes and a nice car – all of it bought with the proceeds of drug dealing. I wasn't brought up in a materialistic home but I discovered that I really liked having expensive things all around me. Where the money came from didn't worry me unless I really thought about it, and I didn't do that very often.

For the next seventeen years I was in that relationship. Although it started off well it was downhill all the way from there. The thing is that if you are in a relationship with a drug-dealer, there aren't very many ways out of it. You know too much. One thing led to another and it all led to cheating and violence. I remember lying in hospital with broken ribs after being beaten up by my boyfriend with Dad sitting beside me asking me where my head was. I heard what he was saying, but the words just didn't get through to me. It was as if they were bouncing off me. And when I was discharged I just went back home for more of the same.

Although I lived off the proceeds of drugs I didn't take them myself. I almost believed that they had nothing to do with me, which says something about the state of my mind. I was low and depressed and sometimes desperate. One night things were so bad that I wanted to take my own life. My boys were teenagers then. I went into their bedroom and stroked their sleeping faces. The tears ran down my face as I asked God to forgive me for wanting to go to sleep and not wake up ever again.

Then there is a blur that I don't want to talk about apart from to say that I was sectioned under the Mental Health Act and zapped by antipsychotic medication. I got it into my head that the hospital was keeping me as a prisoner. That was a bad time.

When I eventually went back home I took Valium to numb how I was feeling and to help me sleep. One day I couldn't get Valium and took Heroin instead and discovered that it took away all my heartache and pain. It was bliss. But if I thought life was bad before, I was to discover that taking Heroin is like selling your soul to the devil. It's the devil's powder. It robs you of yourself and you can never get enough of it; you can never be satisfied. That was when I reached a pivotal moment in my life when one terrible day my younger son spat in my face. 'You can buy yourself Heroin, but you can't even buy me sausages,' he yelled. 'But you're my mum and I still love you.'

A couple of months later, I was overcome by a deep feeling that God could help me. I went to Dad and Mum's church and the pastor told me that what I needed was Teen Challenge. 'You need tough love,' he insisted. That's how I went to Wales to Teen Challenge's drug and alcohol rehabilitation centre. I managed through the programme there with six put-downs for bad attitude and

I gave up my career in shoplifting too. That's all said in one sentence but it actually involved eighteen months of rehabilitation and six months at their School of Ministry – a really, really tough two years. When my pastor said that Teen Challenge specialised in tough love, he was dead right!

I came out of Teen Challenge clean and ready for a fresh start. They even gave me a job as a Teen Challenge support worker in the north-east of Scotland. After ten months of hard graft I was floored by a couple of bouts of flu. Because I was so poorly bloods were sent off and it was discovered that I had Hepatitis C. It wasn't just flu that was the matter with me. The medication I was prescribed was so awful; it made me feel really ill. Totally unfit for work, I went back home to my parents in Largs to be looked after.

Six weeks later, having hardly slept over all that time and feeling utterly desperate, I bought a bag of Heroin and relapsed. When I phoned the centre in Wales for support I was told to get back down there - fast! I did, only to be informed that I'd to go right back to the beginning of the programme all over again. 'Because you've been a staff member,' the Director said, 'we are making an example of you.' I had to do the whole eighteen months of rehabilitation all over again! I believe God used that time to humble me, for it was a very humbling, even humiliating, thing to have to do. To be honest, going through the Teen Challenge programme twice was the making of me.

And that brings me to how I met May. She was down in Largs speaking at my parents' church when I was on a home visit during my second rehab. We had a talk and she gave me her card but I never thought much more about her apart from remembering that she was a lovely wee woman. At the end of my rehab, in 2011, I was wondering what I should do. There was a possibility of going to Leeds, but that would have meant being in a big church and I didn't feel up to that. Suddenly May came into my mind and I knew that I should go to her. 'Do you remember me?' I asked her on the phone. She did. 'I'm looking to come back home to Scotland,' I told May. 'You wouldn't have a spare room, would you?' She explained that Alan was just moving out. 'Give me a week to think about it,' she said, and we rang off. At the end of the week I phoned back and May said that I could stay with her. My dad and mum were so pleased. They'd been praying for me and their prayers had been answered.

I came back up to Scotland and fitted into May's life, though it might not have felt like that to her at the time. She took me to Preshal and I was a volunteer there for a year. I'd had good biblical teaching at the Teen Challenge

School of Ministry but it was May and the others at Preshal who taught me how to minister hands-on to people in need. Nobody taught the hands-on stuff; I just watched May and the others and tried to copy what they did.

Of course, I needed to get a job to support myself. That meant going to college first – another steep learning curve – before I started work with the Scottish Association for Mental Health. I love my work because I love people. I'm involved with folks aged 18 to over 60 who are in self-directed support, basically assisting them with housework tasks, social things and whatever else they want to do. In serving the people I work with I know I'm serving Jesus. Getting a job also meant moving out of May's home. After staying with her for a year she eventually got her spare room back.

If you are wondering about the other people in the story you might like to know that my older son is in his second year training to be a social worker and he has a four-year-old son. My younger son is a successful engineer. Their father is not in their lives or mine. My partner of seventeen years is in prison for murder. Dad and Mum continue to pray for me and support me. And May and Preshal will always be there for me too.

I want to finish my story by saying something about May. Having lived with her for a year I can honestly say that she's the same through and through, she is just full of love. That doesn't make her a pushover, absolutely not. Her love shows itself in anger as well as kindness and in strictness as well as softness. In fact, what she does is reach out through Preshal with tough love to people like me who need it.

6: A Peek into Preshal

When I was young and not in a good place many people helped me. There was Dr Jack Clark, for example, and the thanks he got for coming out to see me when I was drunk and had slashed myself was that I threw whatever I could lay hands on in his direction. Then there were the taxi drivers who delivered me home without having to ask my address because they knew me so well. And, of course, there were the policemen who didn't take me home when I was drunk and out of my mind. They took me through Paisley and into the country and then dumped me so that I'd sober up a bit on the way home. Mum was the best help she could be and little thanks she got for it. My brothers and sisters helped too and without my family I know I'd have lost Tracy and Alan to the Social Services and I would have deserved to. It wasn't help that was missing in my life, it was Jesus.

After I became a Christian in 1981 God put it in my heart to help where I could. Now through Preshal the work of the locusts is being completely restored. Not only do I still have people coming to offer their help, but their help isn't just for me. It's for over 450 women, men and children who come in the door of Preshal. To give you an idea of the helpers we need here's a typical week in our life.

MONDAY
Morning: sewing and card-making.
Afternoon: board games and cooking.

TUESDAY
Morning: art, photography, choir and Bible study.
Afternoon: drums and guitar.

WEDNESDAY
Morning: bowls, pool and dominoes.
Afternoon: cooking and pool.

THURSDAY
Morning: knitting, Bible study, bingo – great for teaching people numbers. A good proportion of those who come in our door have problems with numeracy and literacy.
Afternoon: guitar and sound engineering.

FRIDAY
Morning: literacy and board games – once again, excellent for helping with counting. Afternoon: baking and bowls.

While all this is going on the place is busy with other folk doing their own thing, chatting, getting help with problems and just enjoying having company.

On Tuesdays and Thursdays we have a lunch club which is normally full. By the end of lunch we are all full too. People would be hard pressed to get a nicer meal in a restaurant. I met Iain Graham through our then Chairman, Maclain Service. Iain owns farms including Killochries Fold where highland cattle are bred. He and his wife Sheena provide Preshal with the best of Highland beef. They caught the vision of our people being precious and only the best is good enough for precious people. What we sit down to on Tuesdays and Thursdays is the best steak pies, sirloin steaks, mince and sausages – all of it organic. They also gave us a seven-seater car that allows lads to go down the Clyde coast fishing and so get out in God's good fresh air. That's great for their physical and mental health. Ian and Sheena are examples of the many, many people who are generous to Preshal with their money, time and expertise.

Meet Margaret, she's one of our helpers and she's an expert with a sewing machine.

MARGARET'S STORY

I first heard about May from a friend in the Guild who had heard her speaking at a meeting in Dundee. Preshal was looking for starter packs for people just moving into their homes. We brought some stuff in and you come to Preshal once and the atmosphere is so attractive that you just keep coming back. The first sewing project my friend Cathie Gibson and I were involved with was making a quilt featuring the Preshal logo. Everyone made a block and each one bore the name of the person who made it. It looked magnificent! May sometimes takes it out with her when she's speaking at meetings.

One day Mary Doll, who has been coming to Preshal for years, asked if I could take up the hem of her trousers. I said I wouldn't, but I'd show her how to do it. Cathie and I knew that if we did mending for people, we'd never get to an end of it. But if we showed folk how to do simple things themselves, then we'd have done a useful job. That was the beginning of the sewing group. Mending came first: replacing buttons, hems and even fixing zips. Afterwards we became more creative. Starting with cushions we moved on to quilting, covering coat hangers, making dog blankets and other such things. That was nearly ten years ago and we're still coming!

Knitting was next and before long the click clack of needles was producing scarves and mittens. Maybe it was seeing the wool that made one of the men ask if we could darn his socks. Once again the answer was no, but we would teach him how to darn them himself. I'm sure that till then holey socks were just worn until the holes won the battle against the socks.

One of the staff asked if we could make some puppets. A group of Preshal's adults had written a play and needed puppets to perform it. Now, that really held the attention of the sewing group. These were no finger puppets; they were more like the Muppets you see on television and about half a metre tall. It took us a long time to make them but the sewing group really enjoyed it. They rose to the challenge and we could see a real difference in them, both in their skills and in the sense of satisfaction they had from the work they were doing.

Part of the challenge with the puppets was that they were made to be specific characters because the play was already written. You should have heard some of the suggestions! We got googly eyes for the faces, put lips on them and even managed tongues. That was one of the hard bits. Charity shops were the places to go for scarves and cravats for the finished puppets and in the pound shop we found a variety of wigs. As one of the puppets was meant to be bald, we gave him some long strands of hair to stretch across his bald pate. Another one had to move between being a boy and a girl so he/she can do a quick change of hairstyle when required. These puppets will be used over and over again and I think there are plans to use them in ministry too.

Preshal is a family. There's a real fellowship in the place and a degree of security that many people won't have anywhere else. When people come in there is always someone to talk to and, if some sit on their own, others take note and sit beside them. The other day I noticed a woman looking a bit low. It was her birthday and she was feeling sad. But with company and something to do she was soon back to her old self again. We talk while we work in our wee group and problems are shared. Cathie and I talk about ourselves as well. It's a two-way thing.

May has a heart the size of Scotland and the gift of blending in with any company. What I love is that she can talk about her faith anywhere and to anyone. She's not one bit embarrassed about talking about Jesus. I think her gifts were poverty, alcoholism and drug addiction and she uses her experience of them to help others and to tell them about the Lord.

Some time ago I had an illness and a sad personal bereavement and was off Preshal for quite a long time. May didn't forget me; she kept in touch by phone and prayed for me. She has a big heart to love with, big hands to help folk and big arms to envelope everyone who needs a hug. It's no wonder that we keep coming back!

SHEILA'S STORY

I first met May about five years ago, when she came to our church one Sunday morning to receive gifts from the congregation for Preshal's children. I was a newly retired GP and wondered if there was some voluntary work I might do. As I'd been involved in teaching in Bible class, youth work seemed a possibility. When I came to visit Preshal I mentioned that to May. 'One of our girls has just become a Christian,' she said. 'Why don't you come and do a wee Bible study with her every week?' That's how it started. More people have now been added to the group, though some people have come and gone.

It was quite a challenge finding suitable study material as some members of the group have Bible knowledge and others don't, and not all are competent readers. In the end I decided just to take a passage and look at it together rather than follow a study course. I'm not bothered if only one person turns up because, when that has happened, it has been for a reason; often the one who came had something they needed to talk about.

While we start with a Bible passage, we sometimes find ourselves going off on interesting tangents. Yet God overrules them too. Recently we were talking about Jesus being the Light of the World. From there we found ourselves discussing the occult (I still can't remember how that happened) but it turned out that the occult was a real and live issue for some of the people who were there that day and we discussed issues that would otherwise not have been dealt with.

People choose to come to the Bible study and sometimes choose not to. That's fine with me for we all have off days. It's open to anyone who wishes to come. Not everyone who attends speaks during the study and that's fine too. I can see they are listening. We have some great discussions and I think we all learn from, and are blessed by, our time together. I just pray that God's Word will speak for itself and that those who come will get what they need from it. God is all-powerful and able to do that.

There is nowhere I've ever been hugged as much as I am in Preshal. It took me a little while to feel totally comfortable with that. It's a very safe place and people know they are not judged for what they are or what they've done. Instead, they are welcomed in the door just because they've come in the door. Of course, there are tensions from time to time, but the feeling that people are precious – and treated as such – makes a huge difference. Some don't know why they like coming; they just know they do. I think it is because they are valued, which will be the first time that's happened for a number of them. Having worked as a doctor, I can really appreciate what I see here – disabled people, people who are addicted and people with mental health issues all being treated as people rather than the disabled, addicts or psychiatric cases.

Another lovely thing about Preshal is that it spans the generations. People come in families, several generations of them. That can only help the local community, for everyone round about knows what's going on here. I came along to the Fellowship Meeting one Sunday night. It was a great evening though the music was far too loud for me! But I saw something that night I'd never seen before, young people outside looking in the windows at a service of Christian worship. I think they might also have felt the vibrations of the music!

Having made a few stained glass windows in the past, I wished to use this gift to make a window for Preshal's new building. Many of Preshal's folk have had very difficult, dark lives and I hoped this might brighten their lives a little. I also wished the window to reveal something about God's love and greatness and His power to change lives. It includes a rainbow reminding us of God faithfulness in keeping His promises, a dove of peace, and butterflies which are transformed from caterpillars into such beautiful creatures.

I am very grateful to Mark from the supplier of the stained glass materials in Glasgow, who spent considerable time giving me such good advice regarding certain aspects of the design. I am also really grateful to my joiner and friend, Robert who spent a lot of patient time and careful thought in making the beautiful light box for the window.

I look forward to my visits to Preshal, and always leave feeling encouraged and uplifted by my time spent there.

PAUL'S STORY
Paul's story told by Paul, his Aunt Jan and Tracy, who is his third cousin and carer.

My name is Paul and I'll be twenty-five tomorrow, a quarter of a century! Mum didn't know there was anything wrong with me before I was born. My brother is ten years older than me – ancient! His name is Kevin.

Aunt Jan

Paul was born with lumber sacral agenesis, a very rare condition that means he has no hip, knee or ankle joints, very short legs, no feeling from about the waist down and other problems. It was obvious when he was born that there was a problem and that he'd never be able to walk.

Paul

I was born in a hospital and I spent a lot of time in hospital when I was a child. Because of my condition I catch infections really easily and when that happens I get really ill really quickly. Mum and Dad were good at seeing the signs and phoning for the doctor. I'm now on antibiotics all the time. So that I don't get used to them, the kind of antibiotic changes every month.

I also take seizures and some have been really bad. Once I had a seizure when I was just sitting watching the TV. Mum wasn't sure what to do. When I was in the ambulance going to hospital everyone thought I'd died. They were working on me in the ambulance and then took me to a side room. I was well out of the game and can't remember anything about it.

AUNT JAN

I got a phone call to say that Paul was on his way to hospital so we went right there, my son Allan and me. Paul comes from a very close family of aunts, uncles and cousins and we are all always there for him. That day it turned out that he had pneumonia and we hadn't known a thing about it. It had flared up so suddenly and triggered a seizure. It looked as if the problem was seizures when it was really pneumonia. When they knew what was wrong they could start to treat it.

PAUL

I was at ordinary primary school but I used to fall asleep a lot. In school I had a special Swedish-style chair that I called my throne. Sometimes I gave my teacher a fright. I'd go from sitting on my throne to jumping on to a wide windowsill. I could do that kind of thing then because my arms were so strong. Sometimes when the teacher was reading a story to the class I'd do something like that. I think I was quite mischievous.

PE was one of my favourite lessons because I could do things the other boys couldn't do. I could walk on my hands with my body swinging along. One day I thought I'd show them what I could do and I hauled my way up the monkey bars! I was good at swinging on the gymnastic rings too. Disabled people can sometimes do things that other people can't do.

All my class in primary school went to the same high school. Because I used to get tired I still slept a lot in school. One of my friends, she's called Amanda, did my work for me sometimes. One day the head teacher looked at my book and said, 'There's something wrong here.' Then she looked at Amanda's book and realised that she'd done my work. She phoned Mum. 'Do you know that your son didn't do any work in school today?' she asked. Of course, she couldn't know; she wasn't there! I used to do challenges in school, like challenging myself to eat my soup in record time, and I could do it faster and faster and faster! The teachers just looked at me but the dinner ladies thought I was amazing!

AUNT JAN

Paul has to drink a lot to prevent infections. When he was at school he sometimes didn't do that and we had to keep a close eye on him or he would get very ill. That's been a real problem all of his life. His cousins were at the same school as Paul and they kept an eye on him when he was there and his parents and aunts kept an eye on him when he wasn't at school. He lives with his dad and mum; his mum is my sister. We're a very close family and his Aunt Marie sees him every day.

Something that happened to Paul at school helps to show what it's like for him living with his condition. He used to get out his wheelchair and walk on his hands in PE. Once he got friction burns on his foot from dragging it behind him on the floor. He has no feeling in his lower body so didn't feel it happening. The first anyone knew about it was when it was infected and his mum noticed the infection tracking along a blood vessel. He went to the hospital but couldn't go in the ward as there was an infection doing the rounds. The doctor did an operation on Paul's foot right there and then with his Aunt Marie and my niece watching. Paul didn't need an anaesthetic as he doesn't have any feeling anyway. We were told that he was very lucky. If his mum hadn't noticed it, he could have lost his leg.

Paul

When I left school I went to college to study computing though I missed a year because I wasn't well. After that I went to another college. I like computing. I've got the kind of mind that gets into things like that. My big brother is good with computers too and he knows a bit more about them than me.

My cousin Allan told me about Preshal. Allan was a volunteer for SACRO and one of his service users told him about Preshal. He said it was good and that I'd like it. When I came first I couldn't work out what the place was about. Everyone was so friendly even though they didn't know me. Now I know most people. I should have come here years ago. There are loads of things to do. I'm learning drums but I'm not very good yet. Coming to Preshal is a big thing in my life. Before that I didn't go out much. Aunt Jan and Aunt Marie and the rest of the family were great at coming to see me. They did a lot for me but I like being out meeting other people too.

Preshal is part of my routine now. On Mondays Aunt Jan comes and we go up the town. Tuesdays I come to Preshal and have lunch here. Tony makes great lunches. Wednesdays I go shopping with Tracy at Braehead, she's my carer – and my third cousin! Thursday it's back to Preshal and more good food and good company. On Fridays I go to Tracy's house and have a go on the PlayStation with her son Sean. So you can see that Preshal's a big part of my life. I'm sorry I didn't know about it sooner.

TRACY

I knew about Paul but didn't actually see him until he was about twelve apart from at family parties and things. At a family 'do', when he was eighteen, Paul's mum asked if I would consider becoming his carer. Now he's like a second son to me. Using the funding he gets, *he can choose and employ his own carers. For the first two years he was at college and he loved that. Then he did another year but he was at a loose end after that. There are not many places that have the kind of facilities Paul needs.*

We came to Preshal for the first time in May 2014 not sure what sort of place it would be. There was Paul and me, his mum, Aunt Jan and his cousin Allan. We were certainly checking the place out! We just couldn't believe the welcome we got and how much at home we all felt, especially Paul. The staff are amazing and they come from every walk of life. We know it's a Christian place but it's not preachy at all. Paul and I have both made good friends and we look forward to seeing them every time we come. I meet other carers here too. There's nothing matters at Preshal as much as people and that's what makes it a great place for Paul and me to come. I agree with him; I wish we'd found Preshal years ago.

7: A Message to Malta

Alcohol and drugs are thieves. They steal your health and money. They steal your happiness and sometimes your sanity. And they steal your family life too. They were like locusts in my life. I suppose I had the same potential as other girls my age in Ferguslie Park and the locusts came along and wiped out the lot. There were times when I was left with nothing, certainly not self-respect. Over the years since I became a Christian, God has kept His promise to restore the years the locusts had eaten in amazing ways. One of the ways that He's done that is by bringing people into Preshal who have been where I was, and sometimes in situations a lot worse, and helping them to find themselves and to find Jesus.

THERESA'S STORY

I was thirteen when I met Eddie and he was twelve; I was in first year in secondary and he was still at primary school. We were both looking for love. My father died when I was two and I don't remember him at all. That's sad. What is even sadder was that I don't remember my mum ever giving me a cuddle. She worked really hard doing four different jobs at a time to earn enough to look after us, but she just couldn't cope. I suppose it was because Mum was under so much pressure that she took to drink. It couldn't have been easy for her. I remember going to friends' houses and seeing them with their dads and mums and I just wished our home was different. Eventually the family split up. There were eight of us and the girls went to nunneries and the boys to monasteries. Sometimes we saw each other at weekends.

Eddie was the love of my life. Because he came from a broken home we understood each other. When I went to secondary school he and I used to dodge off school and go to the Queen's Park to play. That sounds stupid but we were really just children. We were married when I was eighteen and had our four children quite quickly one after the other. Eddie was a window cleaner and he worked hard cleaning the windows in the big banks in town. It was a steady job and we had a good life.

I suppose the first I knew there was something wrong was when Eddie started getting out of bed and staring out the window during the night. Sometimes I'd wake up and find him outside in his pyjamas watching the cars going past. Over the next year it was as if I was watching him changing in front of me. I didn't realise he was suffering from serious mental health issues until he began putting a big knife under his pillow at night. When he did that I was terrified to go to sleep. His face changed and his eyes; he wasn't my Eddie any more.

One night I was terrified for the kids' safety and called out a doctor. Eddie was taken into a psychiatric hospital and sectioned. I thought he'd get help and we'd be back to our usual life before long. The kids didn't understand. Edward was six, the twins Julie and Jackie were four and wee Theresa was just two. Every day I went to visit Eddie but he was in a different world from me. He just shouted and cried to get home with me and I had to tell him he'd to stay where he was till he was better. It was heart-breaking.

After about a week I got a phone call to tell me to go up to the hospital right away. 'There's been an accident,' I was told. I took the kids to my sister's house and got a taxi to the hospital. On the way I saw blue lights on the road and I knew in my heart that it was Eddie. That morning he told a nurse that he wanted to take his life as it wasn't fair to me and the kids for him to go on living. When the nurse went to bring a doctor Eddie headed out the window, jumped over a barrier and ran right in front of a car. He was dead before I arrived. I really loved Eddie and we'd been so happy until he took ill.

I went to my sister's house and told the kids that their daddy wasn't going to come home again. That was so hard, but what happened next was even harder. My mother came to Eddie's funeral and her advice to me was, 'There's plenty more fish in the sea. You'll just need to get up and get on with it.'

Eddie's mum wasn't able to help me either because she blamed me for his death. If I'd not agreed to him going into hospital, she thought that he'd still be alive. She didn't understand about the knife and I was never able to tell her that he once tried to kill me.

Before long I moved to a different area and tried to make a new life for myself and the kids. Our house was the cleanest in the block, if not the cleanest in Glasgow. I suppose it was stress that started it, but I soon had Obsessive Compulsive Disorder. I washed and polished and scrubbed from morning till *night. Some nights I'd put the kids to bed in clean sheets and then roll them over in their sleep to change the sheets again during the night. We lived on the third floor and I'd scrub right from the top landing down to the bottom. The neighbours must have thought they were on to a good thing or that I was off my head. I did all I could for the kids. I used to tell them that they were all I'd got and I was all they'd got, and we'd to stick together.*

About four years after I lost Eddie I met a man who took me out after a lot of persuasion as I didn't really want to start a new relationship. He had a good job and a car. After six months I let him move in with me and things seemed to be working out. As I couldn't afford cigarettes I make my own roll-ups. One night he said he'd make them for me from now on. I was still cleaning all the time and he told me to sit down and relax. Later that night I sat down and had a smoke and felt better.

One day, after I had a smoke, I felt really strange but I didn't know what was wrong. I panicked and phoned him. When my partner came back he said he'd something to tell me. 'I've been putting a bit of Heroin in your roll-ups,' he said. 'You're far too jumpy, too nervous. It helps you to relax and it'll help you to sleep.' 'So why do I feel like this?' I asked. 'It's because you're needing a bit more,' I was told. He gave me some Heroin and in two minutes I felt wonderful. I'd not felt so good since Eddie and I were young.

You may find it hard to believe but I'd never actually heard of Heroin. I'd just lived my wee life and that wasn't part of it. Before long I was 'chasing the dragon' and loving it. After the miserable years I'd gone through it just felt so good. About a year later my partner came in and said that he'd had to buy different Heroin and I'd have to inject it. He gave me my first hit and from then on for the next eighteen years I pumped the stuff into myself every day and lost out on my thirties and most of my forties.

My partner bought a house in Cardonald and for the first time in my life I had my own front door. But we were no sooner in when he began to change. He started by putting locks on all the doors of the house, even the inside ones. Then we were banned from some rooms and never knew why. Soon he lost his job and, as we both needed money to feed our drug habits, I'm ashamed to say that we even became involved in armed robberies. And I'm even more ashamed to admit that I left the children locked in the house while we did them.

I'm telling my story in the hope that it will help somebody not to get into drugs, or maybe help a parent to understand their children who are on drugs. Please don't think I'm proud of *what I'm telling you. If I could wash it all out, I would. Taking drugs is like asking a demon to take over your life. And it steals your family too. The twins couldn't wait to be sixteen to get out of the house. At my very worst I was injecting many times a day and taking tablets as well. To get money to feed my habit I sold everything in the house.*

Julie became pregnant and she told me that she and her twin sister were going to move out and find a place of their own as they knew they couldn't trust me with the baby. That hurt like a boot in the stomach. At the time Julie was seeing a boy called Sean who harmed himself. He wasn't the baby's dad. One night Julie and Jackie were going out with their pals and leaving Sean in charge of the baby. He wasn't in a good place and he threatened to thrown himself out the window which was nineteen floors up. 'He won't do it,' I told Julie, for he was always threatening things like that. But he did. My girls were there in front of him screaming their heads off. He was dead when we got down to him. I just put my arms round him. He was seventeen. Sean's mother had put him out the house aged fourteen when she got a new boyfriend and he ended up in a home. That boy had no life at all.

After his death I went to the housing department and asked them to give the girls another flat so that they didn't have to live there. Julie was in a terrible way and took to drink. I was still on drugs and no real support to her at all, though I desperately tried to be. I looked for help in all kinds of places and went to the Mormons, the Jehovah's Witnesses, tried clairvoyance and even spiritualist meetings. Sometimes I went into churches but I couldn't find anything to help me in them. It was at a spiritualist meeting that I met Jas and he moved in with us. When Theresa, my youngest, was fifteen she came home one day and told me she was sorry, but she was pregnant. I said that there were worse things than a wee baby. 'I don't want a baby in here with you and your drugs,' she informed me, and then begged me to go into rehab.

One day I went to a drug crisis centre and spoke to two boys just outside it. 'I'm going to rehab,' I told them. 'You'll not get in there,' they said, and then explained that you had to keep going back and back and back to show willing to make the effort to get free of your drugs. I went anyway. They didn't have any beds, but they said they'd find one for me, and they wouldn't even let me go home to get my things. I think the man knew that I wouldn't come back; he was right. 'Just phone your daughters and tell them you're here and that they can't see you for the next six weeks,' I was told. I did that and they were so pleased.

I stayed and was weaned on to Methadone which meant going to the chemist for it every day. And I was still on it when I went home to Jas after my rehab but I was so, so much better than when I went in because I was off Heroin altogether. By then Theresa had baby Sean and she was staying with her sisters and Julie's baby. About two weeks after I was back home there was a knock at the door at 2 am and we found two policemen who said there had been an accident and Theresa was in hospital. She'd run out of baby milk and a boy had given her a lift to the shop. He was high on drugs and crashed into a roundabout. The driver and the front-seat passenger weren't hurt but Theresa was taken to hospital with a broken arm.

The twins and I went to see her and I was so pleased to find Theresa sitting up in bed. 'Where's the baby?' she asked me, and then told me to look after Sean because she didn't trust anyone else. We left and I went for Sean and took him home with me. Ten minutes later there was a call to say that Theresa was in intensive care. By the time we arrived there she was in a coma and she lay there like that for six weeks. I'm ashamed to say that I started taking drugs again during that time. I didn't know how to cope with what was happening without them. In the end Theresa took a massive heart attack and died.

My heart was ripped out when Theresa died and I blamed myself for everything. I even blamed myself for giving her life. And I blamed myself for being back on Heroin again and Valium too. We moved to a house in Govan, a big rented house, so that Sean could have a garden to play in when he was older. His dad didn't want anything to do with him but his other grandparents did, and they took the baby overnight at weekends. Sean (wee Sean's dad) wasn't allowed into their house because he was an alcoholic.

One Sunday we were at Jas's dad for lunch. My daughter was arguing with two boys outside in the street. Jas went down to break up the fight. One of the boys punched him and, when he fell, they booted him in the head. They ran away when the police came. He was taken to hospital where he had to be operated on for a blood clot on the brain. Jas was never the same man again. His speech was slurred and he'd lost a lot of his memory. He kept saying he'd take his own life and I begged him not to. Things were so bad that I asked Sean's other granny if she and her husband could take the baby for a week. They had a really nice lifestyle and we were in a mess. At the end of the week they wouldn't give him back. She said I was taking drugs and couldn't look after a baby. But I'd promised Theresa that I'd care for wee Sean and I was determined to keep my promise.

I fought to get Sean back and it was so hard. I had to prove all the things I'd done with him from photos, get reports from the nursery and all sorts of other things. Eventually the case went to court. 'If I don't get him back, I'll throw myself in the Clyde,' I told Julie, on the morning of the hearing. I went to the toilet and prayed, 'If you're there, God, please get me this wean.' The judge said the best words I've ever heard in my life. 'Sean will stay with his maternal grand-mother and his other grandparents will be allowed access.' That's when I knew God was there and, although I was still taking drugs, I knew there must be a way forward for me.

Over the next while I stopped taking Valium and cut the Heroin down to one bag a day, and still took my Methadone. One night Jas went out to see his brother and said he'd be back about ten but he didn't come home all night. The following morning his brother phoned to say that Jas had just been found. He'd taken a drug overdose. We'd been together for eight years and he was only forty-two. If it hadn't been for Sean I'd have taken my own life to get out of this mad bad world.

I shut the curtains, didn't answer the door, and just sat inside in despair. When they saw the state I was in the girls took Sean and looked after him. Unfortunately, I was awarded £140,000 after Theresa's death but the money did nothing except bring more misery because I used it to keep every junkie in Govan in drugs. For once in my life I was everybody's best friend. I used to take a hotel room for a week at a time and have drug parties for all my 'friends'.

When I'd wasted all but £2,000 of the money I met a woman who told me that she'd just had a really great holiday in Malta. Going there appealed to me so I decided to blow the last of the money on a holiday. While I was in the hotel in Malta a man kept looking at me. Every time I glanced at him he seemed to be watching me. I thought he was maybe the manager and that he'd realised I was using drugs and was going to put me out the hotel. One day, when I was sitting outside, he came up to me. 'Do you mind if I sit beside you?' he asked. I said that was OK, especially because he had a Glasgow accent. 'I know you're taking Heroin,' the man told me. Then he went on, 'I was once where you are now. But, do you know something wonderful, the Lord Jesus Christ is the one and only person who can set you free from it all.' I shook my head. 'Nobody can do that,' I told him. I really, really wanted to be free of drugs once and for all, but by then I didn't think there was any hope of that ever happening.

The man didn't speak for a wee while and then he said, 'I really believe that the Lord has brought me to sit beside you today and to talk to you.' But I wasn't in a good frame of mind to be talking about churches and Bibles and things, and I told him that. 'Do you know a wee woman called May Nicholson?' he asked. I thought he was changing the subject completely. 'She runs a wee club in Linthouse.' I said that I didn't know her, but that didn't put him off. I believe that God is telling me to tell you about her,' the man went on. 'You go and look up May and she'll welcome you and set you on the right path.' 'Aye, Aye,' I said and May's name didn't enter my mind again.

About five or six years later, when I was in Govan and desperate for a cigarette, I asked a couple for a light and it turned out that they were Christians. He said that they were going to a wee club for their dinner and they'd need to hurry up. 'It's the Preshal Trust we're going to,' the man told me. 'Never heard of it,' I said. 'It's run by May Nicholson,' he commented. Suddenly the man from Malta came into my mind and I remembered May's name from years ago. 'Come with us,' the couple said. And I climbed into their car and got a run to Preshal.

I'll never forget that day. May stood at the door with her arms wide open to welcome me in. Never had I had such a loving cuddle from anyone and I'd not set eyes on the woman in my life before. It was like being wrapped in a warm duvet quilt of love. As usual I was totally exhausted with drugs and just wanted to put my head on May's shoulder and fall asleep. I hope I never forget that safe and loving feeling.

May took me into Preshal. 'Come on through the back,' she said. And when she got me on my own she brought over a big black bin-bag of clothes. What I was wearing was in a right mess. 'See if there's anything in there that'll fit you,' May told me. There were all these clothes! I found what fitted and changed into new jeans and a lovely red coat. When I was leaving May gave me two bags of groceries and said she'd walk me to the end of the road. As we were leaving each other she gave me a £10 note. 'I didn't come asking for money,' I objected. 'I know,' said May. 'If you'd asked, you wouldn't have got it.' It'll sound stupid, but I felt like a deer all the way home. I could have leapt and jumped and skipped along the road. In fact, inside myself that's what I felt I was doing. When Sean came in I showed him my new clothes and told him what had happened. Then I spent some of May's money on fish suppers for us both. I told the girls about it too and they were really pleased for me.

The day before that I'd have spent any £10 note on Heroin but I spent the one May gave me on fish suppers. And from that day to this I've not bought Heroin ever again. I've never even thought about it and that's a miracle. The next morning all I could think about was going back to Preshal and not to get more clothes and money; I just wanted to be there. I threw myself into everything. We play bingo for chocolate bars and I loved winning a bar for Sean. There was a Bible study every week taken by Sheila and it was through it that I asked Jesus to be my Saviour. When I got home later that day all I wanted to do was read the Bible and talk to the Lord in prayer as if He was sitting right opposite me in the room. I started praying for myself and my family and then discovered I wanted to pray for other people too. Prayer felt like a real adventure.

I became really involved in Preshal, which is just like one big family, May's family. Then I went to the Fellowship on Sundays and I couldn't wait for Sunday to come round again. 'My life's really changing,' I said to May, one day. 'The only thing that's holding me back is the Methadone.' She looked at me. 'The Lord healed you from addiction to Heroin and Valium,' she told me, 'and He'll take away the Methadone when the right time comes.' May and Annette, who's a member of staff, prayed every day with me about the Methadone. I went to my doctor and told him that I wasn't going to take Heroin ever again and that I wanted to come off the Methadone too. I did and that was five years ago.

'Do you want to be a volunteer?' May asked me, after I was well and truly settled into Preshal. I told her that I'd love to and I didn't even mind if my job was cleaning the toilets. It turned out that my job was helping Tony, the chef, in the kitchen. I couldn't believe it! Tony is a humble and great man. He's a gentle teacher and never says a bad word about anyone. He taught me how to cook and, if anyone had told me five years ago that I'd be a cook, I'd have thought it was a joke. I used to think I was cursed and that anyone who got close to me would die. Now my life's totally different and I'm not a cursed junkie, I'm a blessed cook!

After I'd been volunteering for a while May said to me one day, 'You're a great wee worker and you keep that kitchen immaculate. How would you like to come and work for us sixteen hours a week and get paid for it.' I thought she was kidding. 'I'm not kidding,' May told me. She took the idea to the Preshal Board and they agreed. I went to the Job Centre and told the girl there that I didn't need their money anymore and that I had a job and wanted to sign off. The girl thought that was brilliant. So did I!

A month after I started Val came into the kitchen and gave me my first Preshal wage slip. It was twenty-two years since I'd worked. 'What's that?' I asked her. I didn't even know how to open a payslip! As soon as I arrived home I ran to the kitchen to get tacks and tacked my payslip to the wall above the fireplace and then sat down on the couch opposite and stared at it. 'Sean, come here!' I yelled, when I heard him coming in the door. 'I want to show you something.' 'What's that?' he asked, when I pointed to the wall. 'That's Gran's payslip.' When he went off to his room to change out of his school uniform I yelled to him to come back and look at it again!

'What's that up there?' Julie asked, when she came in. I told her what it was. 'What's it doing on the wall?' she wanted to know. 'It's there because I want everybody to see it,' I explained. 'And it's staying up there till I get another one to match it next month.' It wasn't the money that was the main thing; it was the peace of mind God had given me. I'm fifty-two now and I feel younger than I've felt all of my life. I didn't know love when I was a child but I'm all loved up as a child of God. When I see addicts in the street I remember what it's like and I know that most of them don't want to do what they're doing and I pray for them.

MAY

Theresa's a slow walker – it took her six years to come to Preshal! When I first met her she was a poor lost soul, just skin and bone and covered with abscesses. One of her daughters told me recently that when her mother changed it made a difference to the whole family. That's what Christ does. I watched Theresa for a long time and could see that she was a hard worker and good with people. She was delighted to be asked to volunteer and put her whole heart into it and now into being a member of staff. I could see a lot of myself in Theresa and knew that if I hadn't been given chances, I'd not be anywhere now.

8: Love in the air

One of the things that the locusts of drink, drugs and self-harm destroyed was my marriage. And if you are thinking that I'm now going to write about a second marriage that turned out happily ever after, you're wrong. However, this chapter is a romance, a Preshal romance. It doesn't begin in a dimly lit restaurant with soft music playing in the background, but in a cell in Barlinnie Prison in Glasgow.

ADAM'S STORY
I was in prison when I first met May. In fact, I was in the suicide cell because I'd given up all hope and had nothing to live for. They are not good places to be, either the suicide cell or that state of mind. So I wasn't interested when someone told me about Prison Fellowship. I'd gone to church when I was young and thought

that I'd ticked off religion, done it, and had worn out the tee-shirt. Prison Fellowship? I didn't want to know. But someone persuaded me to go along and I'm still grateful that I did.

What struck me first was the big number of prisoners who were at the meeting. I'd expected just a handful. I knew some of them were Christians and others were not. May was there – not as a prisoner! Mind you, I discovered afterwards that she'd done her times in prison too. At that point May was going through her cancer treatment, though I didn't know that, and she was wearing a bright red wig and dangly earrings. Although I really wanted to speak to her I didn't have the chance because after the meetings there was always a queue of people wanting to talk to her and prisoners had to be back in their cells sharpish.

I was intrigued by the Prison Fellowship meetings and decided to make the most of my time in jail by keeping company with the kind of people who went to the meetings. That's what started me going to a Bible class in prison and attending church on Sundays too. The Bible class was terrific. A man from Motherwell came every week with his melodeon. There was singing, Bible reading and teaching and I really learned a lot.

When the time came for me to be moved to another part of the prison I decided to keep going to meetings and I did that right until my release. Not long before my release I knew I was still missing out on something but didn't know what it was. Then one day, during a group Bible study, the leader read from Isaiah 55. 'Seek the Lord while he may be found; call on him while he is near. Let the wicked forsake his way and the evil man his thoughts. Let him turn to the Lord, and he will have mercy on him, and to our God, for he will freely pardon.' He looked around and then said, 'This is for someone here but I don't know who it is.' I knew it fitted me but I didn't say anything. The man read the verses again. 'If this means anything to anyone here,' he said, 'please let me know.' I put up my hand and said it was for me. That day I became a Christian.

The Bible study group leaders prayed for me and as they did that I felt like an upturned bottle with everything inside draining out. But reality kicked in within minutes because a prison officer was waiting to take us back to our cells. 'I'm sorry to keep you, Officer,' I apologised, as we went out the door. 'Son,' he said, 'it was worth it.' The man was a Christian and he understood. Imagine that! Even though I was in prison God provided me with a Christian brother to encourage me minutes after I was converted.

As I walked away from the meeting I felt as if I was walking on air and everything seemed beautiful – even the inside of Barlinnie Prison! When I reached the top of a flight of stairs, two big guys looked at me. 'Oh, not another one,' said one to the other. They knew I'd been at Prison Fellowship and saw from my face that I'd been converted. I may also have danced up the stairs because that's what I felt like inside!

At that time I shared a cell with another prisoner.

'What are you on?' my cell-mate asked, when I went in the door.

He didn't remember that I'd been at a Bible study and thought I'd had a visitor who had slipped me some dope! I told him that I'd just become a Christian, that my sins had all been forgiven.

The man reached out and rang the bell. When an officer arrived, he announced, 'I want a move out of here. I'm not staying with this nutcase.'

The officer told him it would do him good. I remembered that there was a Gideon Bible somewhere in the cell and found it, covered in dust, under my bed. For the next hour and a half I read the Bible. I could hardly take my eyes off it.

'OK, tell me about it,' said my cellmate, coming out of his huff.

And I did.

Becoming a Christian completely changed my life but it didn't take away the consequences of what I had done. I still had to finish my sentence but I decided to make the very most of it. There were lots of courses you could do in prison and I tried to do as many as I could, hoping they would help me to get a job when I left. Then I was moved to Kilmarnock Prison and it was from there that I was released.

'There's a crowd waiting for you,' the officer said, as he opened the gate on the day of my release.

He was right. A group of Christians that I'd been writing to since I became a believer were there to welcome me back to the outside world. I'd not met any of them before but I recognised the one who was a minister by his clerical collar. These kind men helped me settle into a temporary place and ordered curry carry-outs for us.

'We'll be back tomorrow,' they said, as they left. And they were.

'Here's the paper,' one of them announced, soon after they came in the following day. 'See what you can find in the "To lets" page.'

'But I can't afford a private let,' I said. 'I don't have any money.'

'All that's been provided for you,' I was informed. I still don't know who gave the money.

We sat down and looked through the small ads.

'Where do you want to live?' one queried.

As I wanted a new start, and didn't like the thought of bumping into people I used to know, I suggested Glasgow or somewhere round about there.

I chose some addresses and my Christian friends took me to see the properties. They prayed over each place we visited and that thrilled me. I'd never seen or heard anything like it. Having decided which one I'd like to live in, we drove to the letting agent to make the arrangement. All went well until the man took out a form with 'Background Report' written at the top of it. My heart sank. Then he looked at the friends who were with me, one wearing a clerical collar, and put the form back in its drawer.

My new friends couldn't have been more helpful. Everything I needed for the flat was provided. I started going round the local churches. When I prayed about which one to go to the Lord seemed to tell me that I was to look for a welcome. Next on my list was a Baptist Church. After the minister welcomed visitors, he said, 'I see we have a stranger here. What's your name?' 'Adam,' I replied. He smiled, 'Welcome, Adam.' So that was the church I chose.

Although I didn't notice her, May was at the service. She remembered me and asked me back to her home for dinner. At that time she was looking for a driver for Preshal work and one of my Christian friends had given me his old car. That's how I became involved in Preshal and how I came to work with May. But it's still not the end of the story.

I drove May all over the country and we shared Scriptures as we travelled. That was a wonderful time for me and I learned such a lot. Prayer became really important and a praying friend suggested I should think about getting married again. My marriage had broken up years earlier. I began to pray about that but not with any great hope of finding someone who would want to marry me, considering I wasn't long out of prison.

At that time Preshal was using a property that belonged to the Disabled Drivers' Club and liked to support them at their social evenings. One night we were there some people were dancing and I danced with a woman called Gloria. She sang to the music as we danced. I really liked that as I'm a singer too. She was a teasing kind of a person and she made me laugh. Next time we went to a social evening Gloria was there again. 'I'm really sorry,' she said to May. 'That was just a carry-on with your husband last time.' 'Husband!' May laughed. 'He's not my husband!'

Gloria started coming along to Preshal, especially to the Sunday evening Fellowship Meetings and that's where she became a Christian. We really liked each other, but I had to tell her my story before our relationship could go any further. I drove Gloria to a viewpoint above Paisley and parked the car overlooking the whole town. 'I've something to tell you,' I said, and poured out the whole story. There was silence for a minute and then Gloria said, 'That's your past and I'm your future.' I couldn't believe what I was hearing. God really did answer my prayers.

Gloria and I were married less than a year later. That was seven years ago and I thank God for her every day of my life. We have our differences, every couple does, but there's nothing insurmountable. We try to talk things through rather than huffing and puffing. And we're both still coming to Preshal, especially to the Thursday morning Bible study. It's great.

GLORIA'S STORY

I was brought up in Clydebank in a big extended family that nearly all lived on one street in the town. That sounds funny nowadays but it wasn't really all that unusual then. As Mum died when I was three and Dad was away at sea I was brought up by Grandma and Granddad. After the war my dad married again and my stepmother was an angel to us. I remember her telling me that she was my new mum, and that's exactly what she was. I was so pleased I had a mum like all my pals.

Like most of the young women I knew I went to work in the local factory and then married when I was twenty-five. Every year for the next ten years I was pregnant and had eight children who lived. Sadly two of them, a boy and a girl, died when they were a few months old. Then my husband died and I was a widow for twenty-two years before I met Adam. It was a real struggle bringing up the children on my own and every year I had to take out a loan to get them school uniforms and it took most of the year to pay the debt back. When I hear how easy it is to take out pay-day loans now, I'm not surprised that a lot of young mums are tempted to take them and then get into awful debt afterwards. Debt is a terrible master.

I went to a wee club in Clydebank and every month we took a bus run over to Govan to the Disabled Drivers' Club for a social evening. There was also a wee sing-song, pies, sausage rolls and a cup of tea, and sometimes a dance or two. That was where I met Adam, though at first I thought he was married to May. When I apologised for being a bit free with her husband, May told me she wouldn't take him as a gift! As Adam and I both like singing, we had that in common right away. I liked him and I could see that he liked me.

Soon after that I started coming to Preshal. Rain, hail or snow I was there, even though it meant two bus journeys and a bit of a walk. I'd never been anywhere like it. People just sat around and talked, and they often talked about Jesus as if they knew Him. I'd never heard anything like it. It was like Preshal was a family and they were all talking about a member of the family. I suppose that's exactly what it is. I began going to the Sunday Fellowship meeting as well and that was where I became a Christian.

Time passed and Adam offered to run me to the bus stop to save me the walk at the start of my long haul home. Soon he was driving me all the way home and having a cup of tea before heading back to Paisley. The day Adam told me about his past was one I won't forget. When he'd finished he said, 'That's my story. If you want me to take you home just say, and we can forget it.' I told him that his story was his past and I was his future. He said, 'Do you mean that?' I assured him that I meant it. What could have been an awful conversation turned into something beautiful.

When Christmas came Adam brought me a parcel. It looked and felt like a big box *of chocolates and I was delighted that he'd given me that. When I took off the wrapping paper I discovered that it was a big Bible! I love reading the Bible and so does he. We were married in the minister's house with just a few others there with us. It was a beautiful service and we were just showered with love. That was seven years ago and I think we are both happier than we've ever been in our lives. Where Adam goes, I go. Where I go, he goes. And where we both love going is Preshal.*

MAY

I didn't lose a driver when Adam and Gloria married, I gained a singer. She has a good voice and sometimes sings at meetings when I go out speaking.

9: Never too Young

When I was at my worst I could have lost my children into the care system and I would have deserved it. Although I loved them to bits I was a rubbish mother when I was drinking, and I mostly was. The locusts of my sin certainly ate years of our family life. Despite that God has restored Tracy and Alan to me in the most wonderful way and I'll never be able to thank Him enough for that. Not only are we really close, but they both work in Preshal alongside me. And they both have great big hearts for Preshal's people.

ALAN'S STORY
I always remember people being about the house, especially after we moved to Dundee when I was in primary six. Mid Craigie, where Mum was a Parish Outreach Worker,

was much the same as Ferguslie Park, only it had the prize for having the worst street in Britain. It felt as if Ferguslie Park went with us as so many folk came to stay at weekends and holidays. I think the walls were made of elastic because we also had people who stayed with us all the time – in our two-bedroom house! Home was a busy place and we all had our wee jobs to keep it ticking over. Life was good, and that's not just looking back; it felt good at the time too. I suppose living in such a busy house with Mum involved with so many people meant that it seemed as if I was living in the centre of the world – and it was quite a world.

One night we heard loads of motorbikes coming along the Kingsway into Mid Craigie and past our house. What a noise they made! It was so loud that a young woman who stayed with us then was so frightened that she grabbed a pillow and squeezed in behind the washing machine! We went to Glasgow once for a weekend and found every window smashed and the inside trashed when we arrived home. It was a case of mistaken identity. The drug dealer who'd done it came back and apologised for getting the wrong address! Not long afterwards his mum and dad's house was petrol-bombed, so I suppose we got off lightly.

When we went back to Glasgow for Mum to work with Glasgow City Mission we'd nowhere to live and moved temporarily into a flat belonging to our friend Cammie. It was so quiet compared to the Mid Craigie house! I got on really well with Cammie's brother and took it seriously badly when he was murdered. Both in Ferguslie Park and Mid Craigie I saw the hard side of life.

I did a number of different jobs and ended up as a supervisor in a bakery. But I was also involved with Preshal as a volunteer pretty much from the beginning, driving Mum about and doing bits and bobs, not one thing in particular. The work in Preshal expanded and, when the Trust was looking for someone to work with the men, I decided to apply. The Board interviewed me and I got the job. That was when the hard work began as I've had to study for certificate after certificate in social care and management. Since then I've worked my way to being Project Manager. The majority of the staff are like me and have come up through the ranks.

Val and I are responsible for fundraising and that's a big job. We have a rolling programme of funders that we apply to each year. Without our supporters, both big trusts and individuals, Preshal wouldn't exist, our building wouldn't have been built and the hundreds of people who come in the door would not be helped. We keep in touch with our funders through e-mails, newsletters and by going to meetings and hope they appreciate the work that they generously facilitate. When people visit us, and many funders do, I think they are pleased to see that Preshal doesn't have 'service-users' or 'clients'; their money goes to help and support Preshal's friends.

To begin with Preshal worked with adults but it was soon clear that there was a need to work with younger people too. We reckoned that 90 per cent of Preshal's friends had children outside in the streets and parks where drugs were rife, gang-fights common and murder was a fact of life. Mum had a vision for youth work and it was decided to run with it. We started by community mapping to see what the needs were and what was already being done. The needs were glaring and we discovered that, while work was being done with young people at the other end of Govan, none was going on where we are.

Our vision was to target twelve to eighteen-year-olds, especially the ones who hung around the local park where gang-fighting was the recreation of choice. We linked with Aberlour Trust for the venture. They did the street work and Preshal took charge of the activities inside our building. On the first night around seventy young folk arrived and over time that settled down to a core of forty to fifty teenagers. One night, when a lad ran in and shouted 'There's a fight in the park!' the place cleared as the whole lot of them – apart from one – were out like a shot to get stuck into it.

The police told us that the crime rate in Linthouse went right down when the youth club was on. One night our Community Police Officer organised a film for us and also brought along a pile of weapons that had been taken in Govan. There were toothbrushes with blades inserted in the bristles, hollow walking sticks with swords inside them and everything in between. Looking at what was there, and thinking what could be done with it, was actually quite sickening. Before showing the film the officer asked for a show of hands of those who'd take part in gang fights. Every hand went up. The film showed the effects of the fights. When it was finished the policewoman asked how the kids thought their mums would feel if they were murdered. Some weeks later there was another call of 'There's a fight in the park!' during a Youth Club meeting and only a handful of the kids ran for the door. We also had someone from the Army come to talk. One boy was keen to join up, but when it was discovered that he was on heavy duty anti-depressants he was told he had to be free of them before he could apply. Imagine a teenager needing *medication like that. He never did get himself fit for the Army.*

Over the years we've taken kids to places like the Scaladale Centre in the Isle of Harris. Now, you can't get more different from Govan than that! The journey was a geography lesson in itself as one of our boys thought we'd reached the English border when we crossed the Kingston Bridge over the River Clyde. Because a lot of kids don't see their grandparents, and many of our older people are just plain scared of the local kids, we decided to take an intergenerational group away for a week. There were ten youngsters and ten older people, including Jimmy, who had his 75th birthday while we were away, and who'd never before been out of Glasgow. They did lots of different things to encourage teamwork; raft-building was probably the favourite. At nights we all sat around and chatted.

One night Mum asked them what their favourite things were and the young folk all said their mobile phones. 'We had mobile phones where we were kids,' she told them. They just laughed at her. 'Yes, we did,' Mum said. 'We used to get two empty tin cans and hammer a hole through the bottoms of them. Then we took a long bit of string and threaded the ends of it through the holes and tied a knot to stop them slipping back through.' The kids all looked bamboozled and the older folk grinned because they knew fine what she was going to say for they'd all had the same 'mobiles' when they were young. Mum went on, 'One of us took one can and the other went as far away as the string would stretch and we talked to each other into the empty cans.' The kids laughed and they took a bit of persuading by the older folk that tin-can mobiles worked! At the end of each day we had a Christian come along and talk to us about Jesus.

One boy was a real pain most of that week. Nobody wanted to partner him at anything and I ended up sharing a kayak with him – me in front and him behind. I was paddling like there was no tomorrow and, when I glanced round, he was lying on his back with his feet up! I explained that we were there to do this together but he wasn't interested. Then he decided to make use of a paddle to tip over the other kayaks. 'Roll us over,' I yelled to the lads in the kayaks nearest us. There were seals all around us and I told the lad in the back that they were the Rottweilers of the sea. The boys tipped us over and the lad went from being a tough man to being a boy in two seconds flat when he landed in the water. I don't recommend this for general use but it did the trick. That lad is doing well now and has a job – no small thing in this part of the city.

While in Harris a teenage boy showed one of the leaders some hash. It was taken from him and Mum tried to persuade the boy to put it in the barbecue fire, but he wasn't having it. He caused a real stramash late one night to get it back. I sent everyone else to their beds and took him outside. After telling him about Harris's night-time wildlife it wasn't too long before he slunk back in. The next morning Mum discovered that the boy was terrified that his dad would hear about it because he (the dad) was a drug dealer. On the ferry back home the lad threw the hash overboard into the Minch. It was really important that he destroyed it himself rather than one of us doing it.

Wee Jimmy was the oldest in the group. The youngsters treated him like a granddad and he loved it. Everyone chipped in and we had enough to buy him a Scaladale Centre hoodie and a cake. Jimmy was in the kitchen and we put the lights out so that he'd get a surprise when he came through and saw the candles on his cake – the first birthday cake he'd had in his life. Jimmy came out the kitchen yelling, 'You've got a power cut. You need an electric card!'

On Sunday we took the group to the High Church in Stornoway; they had done so much to give us a good time and the baking they provided still lives on in memory! Some of the kids were none too keen to go but Mum pointed out the alternatives – peeling the vegetables for lunch or cleaning the toilets. There were no takers for those options! They lads all gave themselves comb-overs (for the uninitiated, think 1930s' straight parting, flattened hair and Brilliantine!). As we came out of church an elderly woman told me that they were like a bunch of angels. If only! The High Church congregation gave everyone in the group a New Testament. One of our lads lost his and there was no peace for anyone till he found it.

As the teenagers we were working with outgrew the youth club we realised that it would be wiser to work with pre-teens, in the hope that early intervention would help break the cycle of drugs – drink – gangs – fights – prison and out on to drugs and drink yet again. That's what we focus on now. Our aim is to produce home-grown leaders for the teenage work of the future. The best folk to help teenagers are other teenagers who've found better things to do and a better life to lead.

Ian, our Youth Development Worker, is involved in work in the centre and also out in the community and local schools. In a local primary school we provide guitar lessons on Thursdays and at one point we had a waiting list of about seventy youngsters! Ian and Annette (who is a Support Worker) go to the secondary school where they work in partnership with the Church of Scotland and the Church of the Nazarene in running a Hot Chocolate Club on Wednesdays where pupils can come and talk. The same partnership runs a Scripture Union group in the school that meets every Friday.

Preshal is a real family; nearly everyone who comes in the door says that. And whole families are involved in helping; even the children of staff members come and volunteer to help with what's going on.

KENNY'S STORY
I first heard of Preshal about six years ago. A friend told me that May Nicholson was speaking at a meeting in Carloway in Lewis, where I live, and I went along to hear her. I've heard a lot of speakers in my day but never one that could hold an audience like May can. She had them laughing and crying, sometimes at the same time. I recognised in May a woman who has a vision for the Lord's work and a real love of people, and someone who can communicate with anyone. Having bought one of her books I left, not thinking that I'd ever see May again.

Some time later my wife Margaret and I heard that our daughter Karis was doing voluntary work with Preshal and we were delighted. May had spoken at her church and Karis liked what she heard and became involved. When I was down visiting Karis I went along with her one Tuesday evening to the Youth Club and found myself playing computer archery with some of the children. I'm involved in youth work in Lewis but we use real bows and arrows in our archery there! May was interested to hear about what we did. I should have realised then that she clocked everything in her mental filing cabinet for future use and I didn't have to wait long before my card was picked out. She asked me to speak at the Fellowship the following Sunday evening.

When the young folk went up to Scaladale Karis was with them and I was invited to help arrange some activities. Since then I've been involved in Preshal in any way I can be, bearing in mind that we live in Stornoway! I'd met Alan before and he'd made a big impression on both Margaret and me. When speaking at a fundraising night in Stornoway Alan said, 'Never look down on anyone unless you are lifting them up. Never judge anyone unless you've walked in their shoes. And never, ever give up on anyone.' We were delighted when Alan and Karis fell in love. Very unusually I sensed that there was something good going on between them before my wife did. That was a first!

Margaret and I have three daughters and they are all Christians and married to Christian men. If we were to thank God all day every day for that blessing, we'd still not thank Him enough. But our life hasn't all been plain sailing. We've known times of very serious illness, even wondering if one of our daughters would survive to grow up. Amazingly God used that time to lead Alexandra to faith and also to bring Karis to the Lord. As a family we've known some very low points and, though I wouldn't choose to go through them again, I thank God for the blessings that came from them. One night Margaret was woken up by this promise for Alexandra, words from the Bible. '"I know the plans I have for you," declares the Lord, "plans to prosper you and not to harm you, plans to give you hope and a future"' (Jeremiah 29:11). And God has been absolutely faithful to His promise to us.

I'm amazed at what goes on in Preshal, at the vision the Board and staff have and the energy and time and love they devote to seeing their vision become reality. I've never been at a Sunday Fellowship meeting when I've not felt God's presence. The prayers said are from deep in people's hearts, sometimes from deep in broken hearts. The Bible tells us *that God hears our humble prayers and there is nothing grand or theological about the prayers offered at Fellowship Meetings. They are humble prayers that go right to God's throne of grace. I'm convinced the Lord is working there, for I see it with my own eyes.*

MAY

I was delighted when Alan and Karis married and thrilled that her whole family is interested in Preshal – Kenny and Margaret along with Mairic Christine and her husband Alexander, and Alexandra and her husband Alistair. It's amazing how God brings people from different cultures (Linthouse and the Isle of Lewis are very different!) to do His work. Margaret and Kenny have their own ministry in Stornoway and I've met people on the mainland who've been deeply affected by it. We have a lot to learn from one another and a great deal of work to do together.

10: An End and a Beginning

Preshal began in 2002 and since then I've watched with wonder at how God has restored the years the locusts had eaten. In my wildest dreams I could never have imagined that we'd be where we are now. For the first six months of Preshal's life God provided everything I needed to live on. After that we were given Social Inclusion Partnership money that helped with rent and Council Tax for workers. While not having an income could be scary I kept reminding myself that, if the cattle on 1,000 hills belong to God, he could certainly provide for me and for Preshal. To start with we rented St Kenneth's Church hall and our equipment consisted of a kettle and toaster from home and tea, coffee, sugar, milk, bread and butter from the local shop. Our activities began in a very small way with decoupage classes and taking some of our people to the nearby Govan Initiative where they joined in computer classes.

I wasn't on my own; Maclain Service was my right-hand man. We had worked together before that and shared the vision for what Preshal could do for the people of Govan. I'd met many men over the years, but Mac was the first gentleman I ever met and he's a gentleman still, despite working with me all this time! I remember sitting in the vestry of St Kenneth's Church with the minister, David Keddie, and Mac trying to fill out forms for funding when none of the three of us even understood the questions! We must have done something right though because we were given funds.

When we discussed a name for the project we knew we were looking for something 'different', but what? It was Mac's wife Jo who suggested Preshal – the Gaelic for 'precious'. My spirit rose to the suggestion right away. It was certainly different but it was also a conversation starter. 'Preshal? What's that?' gave us the opportunity to say that we aimed to show people that we are all precious in God's sight. David Keddie caught that vision and he, along with Mac and me, ran with it. Mac had just retired from business to enjoy a quieter life. Thanks to Preshal his retirement has been busier than his working life was.

He became our Chairman and has only just retired from that position though he's still a Board member. Mac and Jo have supported us all the way and still do. I sometimes think that I'm a bit of a rough diamond and Mac is a pearl. We're light years apart but complement each other really well.

Not long afterwards I was asked to speak at Drymen Parish Church Guild. After I'd given my talk we had a cup of tea and I started to talk with a lovely woman. As she knew about me from the talk, I asked her to tell me about herself. She told me how she became a Christian. While she was speaking I discerned that my new friend was shy when talking about her faith and asked her about that. Sadly she agreed that I was right and explained that she didn't want to force her beliefs on anyone and put them off altogether. From what I had learned of her story I knew others would be interested and told her so.

A wee while later I went to the ladies' room. 'Do you know who that was you were talking to?' someone asked me. 'It was Cathy,' I replied. My companion smiled. 'That's Cathy, Duchess of Montrose,' I was informed. Cathy and I got on so well that night that she invited me to her home, telling me that she had a friend she'd like me to meet. It turned out they both had a powerhouse of fundraising skills. Their first major effort was to hold a coffee morning and ask for donations of tea, coffee and bread for toast for Preshal. Then they organised a meal for 150 people at which a wonderful homeless busker provided the entertainment. Having Cathy on board was a huge encouragement to Preshal and we were all thrilled when she agreed to be our president.

When the time came for us to leave St Kenneth's Church hall we moved just a short distance to a building belonging to the Disabled Drivers' Club. It was one big hall with a tin roof and basic toilet facilities. The whole area was surrounded by barbed wire to keep people out. We knew right away that gave the wrong message and that, when we had our own building, there wouldn't be any barbed wire in sight. We wanted people to come in, not to keep them out! The premises weren't exactly versatile but we put them to good use. We added an office and a store – both windowless shipping containers that we put alongside the hall. In that building we saw people getting off drink and drugs and families being restored. There was a four-ringed cooker and meals for eighty were made on it. We also ran cooking classes with 'all in one pan' meals being made on gas rings set on table tops along the side of the hall. It was great when folk came in and told us they'd made the same meal again at home.

Four computers were bought and our first IT classes were held in the shipping container that we used as an office. The 'office space' was the size of a toilet!

Cathy was a duchess but she was also a friend to Preshal's people. They knew her as Cathy; she knew them by name. And she wasn't afraid to roll up her sleeves and muck in or to put on a wig and perform. A wig? Line dancing has always been a popular activity. In fact, that's sometimes what brings people in the door. One day Cathy and a friend were there when the line dancing music started up. Both put on bright coloured wigs and joined in with the rest of them. Imagine what it means to people who have little or nothing, or who feel unwanted or useless, to have a duchess and her friend dance with them and then sit down beside them and share tea and hot toast.

One day a woman came in whose husband was in hospital. 'Could you sign my benefit book?' she asked, because her man usually did that and he wasn't there. It turned out that she couldn't do it herself because she wasn't able to read and write. A man used to come in every day with his newspaper. It was only when we noticed it was often upside down we realised that he couldn't read either. They were the inspiration for us starting literacy and numeracy classes. One of our friends, she's called Mary Doll, couldn't read and she too did literacy with us. Now she's able to read her Bible and even to do the reading at our Sunday Fellowship. At a big meeting in the Drumossie Hotel Mary Doll read her favourite psalm. I don't think there was a dry eye in the room.

We began to see people becoming Christians, people who were totally unchurched and who would have found church a really difficult place. 'Would you mind if we start a wee fellowship meeting on Sunday evenings?' I asked my pastor, assuring him that we weren't planting a church. He gave us his blessing and the Fellowship began. I go to my own church on Sunday mornings and am fed richly there and then I go to the Fellowship in the evening. I first met Cathy at Drymen and Preshal has built up a relationship with the church there. We've had a group of Drymen people come to our Sunday Fellowship Meeting with Cathy and each Good Friday, Preshal goes to Drymen and takes a service there. All these things, and much else besides, took place in that hut with its tin roof and shipping container office.

Cathy and I became like sisters and loved each other dearly. She went with us to Northern Ireland to meet up with Tom Kelly, one of the Bogside artists. Tom invited her to unfurl a peace banner. That was really appropriate as Cathy had been involved in peace and reconciliation work through

Moral Rearmament ever since she became a Christian. In fact, it was through the travelling that work involved that she met Seumas, Duke of Montrose, whom she married. During the visit to the Bogside Cathy was presented with a beautiful vase which she kindly gifted to Preshal.

I knew Cathy would understand the conflict in Northern Ireland. One night I had a barbecue in my garden. The Duke and Duchess of Montrose were there, and their son Ronnie, along with people from Palestine, Lebanon and the Bogside as well as some of our very own Govanites. As the evening wore on both Cathy and Ronnie talked a little bit about their work in reconciling peoples with peoples. It was amazing how similar the feelings expressed were, despite the very different backgrounds. The discussion was all about allowing people to talk, really listening and being big enough to forgive. Not only did Cathy understand the troubles in the Middle East but she also understood the Irish conflict and the sectarian problems that appear in Govan from time to time.

At first we rented the Disabled Drivers' Club building and then bought it, all the while dreaming of a day when we might have a purpose-built home. Lawrie Shanks, the mother of one of our Board members, died and her family gave us money from her estate that was kept as the first instalment of our new building. Some years passed and funds were raised in all kinds of ways. Money came in single £1 coins and sometimes in thousands but the £1 was always just as precious as the £1,000, and sometimes given more sacrificially. I remember an elderly woman giving me £1 for the work of Preshal and saying that wouldn't go very far. God, who fed 5,000 from a few loaves and fishes, fed 90 friends their breakfast with her £1 coin, giving each of them two slices of toast with their morning tea.

We had the bulk of the money we thought we would need before work on our new premises began. Sir Alex Ferguson was Patron of our new building fund – and everyone had heard of him! Somehow it was very sad handing over the keys to the shipping containers to their new owners. How can you become emotionally attached to windowless, airless shipping containers? I don't know, but we did! It was also sad – but exciting - seeing how quickly the building was demolished. Of course, we had to find somewhere to 'live' in the meantime. Our first home was a disused nursery which Johann Lamont, our local MSP, found for us at the other end of Govan. It was fine, though small, until just after Christmas when some lads trashed everything in it and set it alight. Thankfully we had delivered Christmas presents to loads of children just before that or they'd not have had

Santa. The worst of it was that we had to close for a few weeks at a time of year when many people are especially lonely and sometimes cold and hungry.

Looking back on our time there even the fire had blessings in it. Preshal's people travelled to Linthouse to the nursery and now some who first met us at the nursery travel to our new building and have become part of our family. They likely wouldn't have heard about us had we not gone to live with them for a time. The fire was on the first Sunday of a new year and we had decided, for once, not to have a Fellowship Meeting. If we had, whoever had gone to open the door would have disturbed the break-in. From the violence of the damage that was done it's quite possible that a murder might have been committed. Most of what we lost in the fire was replaced by our insurers and what was not was bought from donations.

ALAN
The building couldn't be secured after the fire and I sat outside it in the car all night. I'm not quite sure what I thought might be stolen as the trashing was seriously thorough! Members of our staff were wonderful over the six or seven weeks we were homeless. They met up with people in cafes and visited them in their homes. Val and I filled in applications for funding in a Char Grill!

Of course, we needed to find another new home and that turned out to be Shieldhall and Drumoyne United Free Church hall where we were accepted with warm hearts and welcoming arms open as wide as the Clyde. 'Use what you need,' we were told, 'and we'll move things to wherever suits you.' And they meant it. The building was so suitable that, if we'd not been in the process of getting our own place built, we might have been tempted to stay there. We were so welcome and so at home and we're still indebted to the people there, especially the minister Robert Ralston, who along with Gus and David couldn't have done more for us. They didn't even mind us digging up part of their grounds for a gardening plot. And they're still helping. We had so many people at our Christmas dinners last year that we had to borrow their chairs!

We discovered that we needed £75,000 to complete the new building. One night God woke me up during the night with the words, 'You have not because you ask not' and the name of a man came into my mind too, someone I'd never met. I went to see him and we talked about our backgrounds; we'd both been brought up in tenements and they have a life of their own. Without even asking to see Preshal's accounts, he said he'd give us the final £75,000. Done! Praise the Lord!

11: Home

In November 2013, before the official opening, we had a special Sunday Fellowship. We wanted the building's life to begin with what matters most. Our friends in the United Free Church were there and other friends and supporters too. Brian Souter brought a message from God's Word which was very appropriate as he and his wife Betty have been good friends to Preshal over the years.

On the big day our new building was opened by the Duke and Duchess of Montrose, or Seumas and Cathy as they are known to their friends in Preshal. Ian White, singer and songwriter, came along with his guitar and helped all who crowded in to praise God for His wonderful goodness. We were really pleased that an encouraging number of those who had helped fund the building were there to see it completed. It was just exactly what we wanted.

Come with me and I'll walk you round our home. When we go in the door there's a reception area in front of you. Wee Jimmy looks after it. Remember wee Jimmy, who was seventy-five during our inter-generational trip to Harris? There are lovely toilet facilities off the entrance hall. The hub of the place is our main hall which is big enough to have our pool tables, plenty of chairs and tables to sit around and use for activities and still leave room for eighty to be fed lunches twice a week in the middle! It's just great for our Sunday Fellowships as well.

The kitchen is off the hall and Alan wants me to say that's the hub of Preshal because so much happens there, but for me the hall is the hub. Maybe Alan says that because the way to a man's heart is by his stomach! We have a full training kitchen and Tony is in charge with Theresa right behind him. As well as cooking our meals Tony runs cookery and baking classes. There are many people in Preshal who couldn't make a meal who can now cook for themselves and get pleasure from cooking as well as eating what they make.

At the opposite end of the hall from the kitchen we have a door to our storage area – no more shipping containers here! The last door off the hall leads to Preshal's office, with

Val in charge and with two other desks for Ian and Alan, Annette and me to share between us. Across the corridor we have toilet facilities, including facilities for our disabled friends. Along from that there is our general purpose room, and it really is general purpose – holding group activities including Bible study, sewing, crafts, guitar lessons, literacy, numeracy and much else besides. It's not possible to give an exact list of activities because, apart from the core ones, they change according to need, the availability of leaders and the time of year. For example, we might focus on Red Nose Day for a whole week!

Opposite that we have the Lawrie Shanks Room, that's our quiet room. We didn't have a room like this in any of our previous homes and it's a huge blessing. It's used for counselling individuals, couples or small groups. Eric, one of our volunteers, is there each week with one-to-one or small group Bible studies. Among the people Eric draws alongside are some with low literacy skills. He even found a large-print Bible for one of Preshal's friends who is visually impaired. The Lawrie Shanks Room is also used as a crisis room when someone has an urgent need of support or even to cry in private.

We were a little bit worried that our new building would feel clinical compared to the homeliness of the other places we've been in but that just hasn't happened. I think that's because Preshal is people rather than a place. Although many of our dreams have been realised some are still in dream form. For example, we have an area beside our car park which, if you close your eyes and use your imagination, is the Catherine Montrose Memorial Garden filled with vegetables grown by Preshal's friends to be cooked in our training kitchen and eaten at our Tuesday and Thursday lunches. You'll see in your imagination that we've plenty left over and that will be taken home by our friends to help feed their families using cookery group recipes. We hope this dream will materialise in the near future. Now, you've had a virtual tour of Preshal and I hope you'll come and see it for yourselves.

When you come you'll meet Preshal's people, now they ARE the heart of Preshal and there's nobody going to argue with that. Among those you'll meet are the staff who've already been mentioned and Kim, Alison, Andy, Tracy and Eleanor, our support workers, and Lindsay who works with young people and is our worship leader. They not only support those who come in Preshal's door, they also support each other.

There's a passage in 1 Peter 2 that talks about us being living stones. Psalm 127:1 tells us that unless the Lord builds a house, those who build it labour in vain. And Jesus says a wise man building a house digs deep and lays a firm foundation. In a new building it is important that you dig the foundation deep and set boundaries because the people that we work with have often never had a firm foundation or had any boundaries set in their lives. What would life be like if there were no boundaries? It would be chaos. The work we are involved in is difficult because we have to dig right down to the foundations and it is hard ground, but the rewards are great. To see families that were broken finding new life through Christ is wonderful. More and more people are in need of help and support, and it is only through our new building that we are able to expand our work and reach more people for the Kingdom of God.

The real building that we want to construct is made from living stones. Some are damaged, chipped, cracked and mis-shapen, but these are the stones that we love and work with. Every one of them is precious and has a place in the design. Our building is laid on the greatest cornerstone, which is Jesus. Developed around this cornerstone are all the different types and shapes of stones – people who are, or have been, drug addicts, alcoholics, gamblers, ex-offenders, gang members, disaffected young people, those who have suffered mental illness, been lonely, homeless and broken and, of course, the stones which are classed as normal, if there is such a thing as being normal. All these stones are fitted together to form a welcoming home, not a castle.

Cement is crucial in the erection of a building as it holds the stones together. Our cement is made of compassion, empathy, support, help, a listening ear and understanding. But the greatest ingredient in the cement is love. You can have everything else there but, if you don't have love, the building will not stand.

Windows are a vital part of our building. They allow the light to shine into the dark areas of depression, bereavement, broken relationships, low self-esteem, lack of confidence, loneliness and poverty. When the light shines through the windows it brings about a sense of hope, joy and peace. It dispels the darkness. It helps people to see another way of life and a light at the end of their dark tunnels. That light is Jesus because He is the light that guides our lives.

The roof provides shelter, safety and protection. When the storms of life come, and not one of us can say we have not been in a storm, we are protected by the roof. Storms affect everyone, not just people with drug or alcohol addictions, those who are homeless or bereaved, lonely or suffering from physical or mental health issues. It is in storms that the roof becomes a blanket of God's love, a cover to provide a refuge under which we draw strength from one another and share a sense of security. God's love is for everyone.

Preshal's door is open, it's not locked. Everyone is welcome whether they come from a prison or re-hab, an empty house or the streets. There is no entry fee or dress code. The Gospel tells us that salvation is a free gift and as people enter our building they have the opportunity of finding the greatest gift of all. In and through the Lord Jesus Christ we are able to offer forgiveness for whatever is in the past, and the promise of new life and a clean slate, a completely new beginning.

We seek to look after our stones, caring for them and feeding them both physically and spiritually. It is a joy to work with the cracked, chipped and broken stones. We watch as God polishes, hones and shapes them into something beautiful. As he transforms them they sparkle for others and stand firm, becoming pillars of the community and lights that shine out into the darkness drawing other people in to experience the light of God in their lives.

After the new building opened a new work began to develop when disabled people started to come along, both those with physical disabilities and others with learning difficulties and mental health issues. Some come with carers who enjoy meeting up with each other and relaxing together. We've been told by several people that they've looked for years for a place like Preshal and not found anywhere until now. Our disabled friends come from different parts of Glasgow and from Paisley too. The cooking class now includes people who are in wheelchairs who are helped by their carers. I expect this work to grow further as news of it spreads by word of mouth. Providing facilities for people with special needs sometimes attracts funding specific to their needs. Our problem is finding funding for run-of-the-mill things like electricity and toilet rolls!

It is often in the Sunday Fellowship that we hear most clearly how our precious people are getting on and what's troubling them. Because they are unchurched they aren't inhibited by conventions. People share their worries and we all pray for them. And it's not just staff members who pray, Preshal's people pray for each other. Sometimes my heart's all but broken when I listen to what's said and I know God hears the sometimes tortured prayers that are offered to Him.

The Fellowship's music is provided by our own home-grown band. Playing an instrument or singing isn't necessary for becoming a member of Preshal's staff, but God seems to have brought gifted people to us. Lindsay does youth work and doubles as singer and songwriter. Tony plays the drums as well as wielding wooden spoons in the kitchen. Ian, our Youth Development Worker, plays bass and Alan plays guitar, sings and writes songs as well. The general purpose room is also a recording studio and that's where Oran Ur, Preshal's first CD, was perfected. Lindsay's daughter Liath plays saxophone and Alan Docherty does the technical stuff.

We have a speaker every Sunday at the Fellowship and speakers have to be prepared to answer questions as a discussion-cum-question time follows the talk. Absolutely anything can be raised, some real puzzlers. Who did baptise John the Baptist?! Speakers have to be fairly flexible and to accept us as we are. Not everyone's attention span lasts the whole meeting and occasionally that's very obvious – like the night we were sitting praying when a voice rang out asking if anyone wanted to buy a washing machine and tumble dryer. I don't know if there were any takers!

Although Preshal is open from 9.30 am till 4 pm five days a week, Preshal's people are precious every hour of the day and every day of the week. If we hear of a problem, we'll always try to go the extra mile. I remember one of Preshal's friends, who had been a drug addict, started using again when she hit a really stressful patch. Someone told Alan that Susan (that's not her real name) was wandering around the streets. Alan and Karis found her, took her to their home and one or other stayed up with her as she endured a very distressing psychotic episode and paced the floor all night.

I was away but, when I came back, we heard that Susan was out wandering again, a poor lost soul, even walking along the motorway. Alan and I searched till we found her and brought her home to me. Shona was staying at the time and she and I bathed Susan and cut her hair. The next day we bought her new clothes. So when we took her to the psychiatric hospital Susan was clean, tidy and well dressed. I explained her condition and was told that they would not take her in even when I said that Susan wasn't a danger to anyone else, but she was certainly a danger to herself as she'd been walking along the motorway. Even in my drinking days I'd stand up for the underdog and I wasn't going to let Susan down. She was eventually admitted and it was three months before she was fit to go home. Susan now lives in a different part of Glasgow and she's doing really well. We still keep in touch with her and she knows we're here for her.

Preshal is not only for the people who can come to us. Preshal's friends are all over the place. They are folk we've met when we've been fundraising or out speaking at meetings. It was at a meeting in Ayr that I met Jim.

JIM'S STORY
When I moved to Ayr almost exactly a year ago to try to get a new start after years of alcoholism, I'd no idea how much of a new beginning it would be. My one friend in Ayr was Bea, who is a Christian, and through her I met Rory and Kirsteen, her minister and his wife, the day I arrived. The very next day Rory led me to the Lord and the following day I went to church. What a welcome! It was a small congregation and news of my conversion had everyone buzzing, myself included.

It's never easy to get off drink but I had a huge amount of support and that helped. Life was so different. I had new friends in church and within weeks I was doing voluntary work that I knew was useful. Life was really good. Eight months later our church arranged for May and a group from Preshal to come down and take a meeting with a view to establishing a Road to Recovery group in Ayr. It was a wonderful evening of testimonies and it was great to meet May, having read both the books about Preshal. Road to Recovery met for the first time the following week and it's doing really well. I went up to visit Preshal and was blown away by the loving acceptance I met there.

Just weeks later I began to struggle. Life was very busy and there was a possibility of a job coming up. I let everything crowd in on my closeness to Jesus, and the newness of being a Christian and a member of a loving fellowship had begun to wear off. In a way I'd become used to it. Out the blue I developed a really bad chest infection and found myself in hospital. When I was discharged my mind was in a mess and I started drinking again, just for a few days, but I felt like scum. I'd let God down. I'd let everybody down. But my Christian friends were there for me with prayer support and really tough love.

Since then it's been hard. A friend let May know that I was going through the mill and she phoned and helped me in a bad patch. I'm really struggling these days, even to take it a day at a time, and I don't always make it. I can understand what Preshal means to those who can go there often. That must be such a help. I'm so grateful for my Christian friends who support me in prayer and who encourage me with texts and phone calls and visits. They know I need them but they've no idea how deep that need is just now and how desperate I am sometimes. I really do cry to God, with real tears.

*I visited Preshal again very recently and the
love there was wonderful. May asked me if I'd
share my story to show that Preshal doesn't
just care about the people who go in the door.
Preshal's friends are all over the place and just
at the end of the phone.*

Ayr is down the Firth of Clyde and, for many
years now, Preshal has had its own special
place on the Clyde coast. Before Preshal began
a small caravan was bought at Saltcoats, just
across the road from the shore. Gradually
over the years it has been upgraded, thanks
to many generous gifts, and now it's a lovely
eight-berth caravan that can take as many as
three families – provided that's three single
mums with children. We leave food in the
caravan and pails, spades and other seaside
stuff so that the little money they have can be
used for treats.

Many of Preshal's kids don't get holidays
and you should see their faces when they
come back from a week in the caravan. Their
eyes are like stars and they dream about their
holiday there next year from the day they
come home. The caravan is so well used that
the staff can't get there. School holiday weeks
are taken up with families. Pensioners go at
other times and people with problems who just
need to get away use it too. Just occasionally
I've been overnight with some pensioners.

What does that say about my age! Sometimes people talk about 'May's caravan'; I tell them it's the Lord's caravan, and so it is.

Cathy was diagnosed with cancer and, when she told me about it, we both thought she'd get better. But it wasn't to be. She still came to our meetings until a couple of weeks before she died. One morning Seumas phoned to say that his wife had been taken to hospital. I went in to see Cathy and prayed for my dear friend. When the nurse said that the family had been sent for I knew the end was near. Because we both understood that, we had the privilege of saying what we wanted to say, of thanking each other for our friendship and for all we'd done together. Cathy told me that she was ready to go and I could see that was true.

As we talked about meeting again in glory, I thought how wonderful it was to see someone as ready to go home to Jesus. I left knowing that I'd not see my friend again on earth. Cathy died not long afterwards with her family around her and with these words from the Bible being read as she passed from life, through death, to eternal life.

> '...I know whom I have believed, and am persuaded that he is able to keep that which I have committed unto him against that day' (2 Timothy 1:12 KJV).

Looking back I can see that I learned many things from Cathy but one is especially precious.

I talk to God in prayer; I love praying, but until I met Cathy I didn't stop talking long enough for God to speak to me. After reading her Bible and praying, she would sit in silence listening to what God had to say to her heart. She didn't listen for words in her ears but for blessings and leadings, for confirmations of the rightness of things or for indications of their wrongness. Cathy was a wise woman and her wisdom came from God's Word, from prayer and from much waiting in silence on the One she loved.

Another thing I learned from Cathy was about marriage. Although Seumas was in the House of Lords and away from home most weeks, and often for extended times, she didn't live an individual life. She always discussed issues with him before coming to decisions. Cathy was deeply involved with Preshal, and with other things besides, but first and foremost she was Seumas's wife, Hermione, Ronnie and Jamie's mother, and Grace and John's grandmother. She saw it as her role under God to serve them and then to serve others. I can honestly say that Cathy was the most servant-hearted person I've ever had the privilege of knowing. And I see her mother in Hermione, who has taken Cathy's place as Preshal's President. We are most grateful to her.

On the day I became a Christian God promised to restore the years that the locusts of drink, drugs and self-harm had stolen from me and He has kept His promise hundreds of times over. He's kept His promise in my life and in the lives of Preshal's friends. He's restored Theresa and Martin, Shona and Adam and many, many others. It's my prayer that God will use this book to touch your heart and to begin a work of restoration there. Jesus says,

> 'For God so loved the world that he gave his one and only Son, that whoever believes in him shall not perish but have everlasting life' (John 3:16).

Anyone wishing further information about the Preshal Trust should contact:

The Preshal Trust,
PO Box 7344,
8 Aboukir Street,
Glasgow,
G51 4QX

email: preshaltrust@hotmail.com
Tel: 0141 445 3689